THE SHERMAN TANK

ROGER FORD

THE SHERMAN TANK

ROGER FORD

MBI Publishing Company

This edition first published in 1999 by
MBI Publishing Company,
729 Prospect Avenue, PO Box 1, Osceola,
WI 54020 USA

The information in this book is true and complete to the best of our
knowledge. All recommendations are made without any guarantee on the part
of the author or publisher, who also disclaim any liability incurred in
connection with the use of this data or specific details

We recognize that some words, model names and designations, for example,
mentioned herein are the property of the trademark holder. We use them for
identification purposes only. This is not an official publication

MBI Publishing Company books are also available at discounts in bulk quantity
for industrial or sale-promotional use. For details write to the Special Sales
Manager at Motorbooks International Wholesalers and Distributors,
729 Prospect Avenue, PO Box 1, Osceola, WI 54020 USA

Library of Congress Cataloging-in-Publication Data Available

ISBN 0-7603-0596-X

Printed and bound in The Czech Republic

Editorial and design by
Brown Packaging Books Ltd
Bradley's Close
74-77 White Lion Street
London N1 9PF

Editor: Chris Westhorp
Design: Wilson Design Associates

Picture credits
Robert Hunt Library: 2-3, 6-7, 8, 9, 56, 64-65, 74, 77, 89
Tank Museum Collection, Bovington: 17, 23, 24, 25, 26, 26-27, 34, 34-35, 36, 37, 38, 39, 40, 41,
42, 43, 44, 45, 46, 47 (both), 79
TRH Pictures: front cover (both), 10, 11, 12, 14-15, 16, 18, 22-23, 31, 48-49, 50, 51, 52, 53, 54,
54-55, 56-57, 58, 59, 60, 61, 62-63, 66, 67, 70, 71, 73, 76-77, 81, 82, 86, back cover

Artwork credits
Aerospace Publishing: front cover, 20-21, 68 (both), 69 (top)
John Batchelor: 28-29
Bob Garwood: 69 (bottom), 84 (both), 85 (both)
Ray Hutchins: 32-33

Pages 2-3: M4 Shermans pass dead horses and German equipment during
the push towards Avranches in July 1944.

CONTENTS

CHAPTER 1

Genesis of the Sherman

Before the US Army could begin to develop an armoured force, post World War I, it needed to establish a meaningful requirement and decide just what sort of vehicles it needed. However, the development process itself was hampered by a lack of commitment to the very concept.

The United States Army formed a tank corps in July 1917, 10 months after the first lumbering, barely battleworthy British Mark Is went into action on the Somme front. In those days, it took a very dedicated tanker to affirm with any conviction that this was the shape of things to come, but by the time American troops joined the ground offensive, in September 1918, armoured vehicles formed an important part of their order of battle. They were British Mark IVs and Mark Vs and lightweight, two-man French Renault FT17s, originally known as 'Six-Ton Specials' and later as the M1917; and already the design of an Anglo-American heavy tank, the 40.6-tonne (40-ton) Mark VIII, known as the Liberty or International, was well under way in the United Kingdom as plans for the 1919 Offensive, which was to have employed no less than 4000 of them, were being drawn up.

EARLY DESIGNS

There were indigenous designs put forward in the United States, too – for the Holt Three-Wheeled Steam Tank; for a vehicle based on the British Mark IV but much larger, also powered by steam (and with a flame-thrower, then just becoming a practicable weapon, as its main armament), devised by the US Army Corps of Engineers, and for a skeleton version of the Mark IV, conceived as a light tank with good trench-crossing capability – but all these projects were cancelled in 1918, after just one prototype of each vehicle had been built. The only American tank to go into production was a light vehicle, officially described as a machine gun

Left: From its combat debut at El Alamein in late October 1942, the Sherman saw action in every major theatre of operations in World War II. This British M4 is disembarking from an LCT at Anzio, in late January 1944.

carrier, based on passenger car components: the Ford Three-Ton Tank. It was powered by two 20bhp engines derived from that of the Model T passenger car, and managed a respectable 13kmh (eight miles per hour); it had a crew of two, and a single Browning machine gun (arguably America's most important contribution to the technology of World War I), and 15,000 were ordered in all. Just one-tenth of one per cent of those had actually been delivered at the time of the armistice, whereupon the programme was cancelled. A development of the Three-Ton Tank, the Ford Three-Man Tank, was also cancelled after trials in 1919. In addition to the 15 Ford tanks, 952 M1917s, extensively re-engineered, were built under licence (out of 4000 originally ordered), and 100 Mark VIII tanks were assembled (from parts manufactured during the war) at the Rock Island Arsenal between 1 September 1919 and 10 June of the following year. This was to be virtually all the US Army had in the way of tanks until the late 1930s, and there was no dedicated infrastructure to deploy them, for the tank corps was disbanded in 1920, and all its vehicles were re-allocated to the infantry (the procedure was carried out by act of Congress, so it had the force of law). Tank development in the USA was thus in grave danger of stagnating entirely, but thanks to the inauguration of what was nominally a policy study group, the Tank Board, in 1922, at least a rump remained – and very important it was to prove.

In fact, the board was more than a policy-making body; it had the power to order the construction of prototypes to ·test its theories of design and development, and was also to

be instrumental in maintaining a cadre of trained tankers. It decided to concentrate development on light- and medium tanks, the former in the five-tonne range and capable of being transported by truck, and the latter limited by the 15.24-tonne (15-ton) capacity of the US Army engineers' bridging equipment. The light tank development programme was abandoned in 1926 and the existing M1917s kept in service instead, though it was reinstated later and a much bigger vehicle was developed and went into service as the Light Tank, M2, in the late 1930s; and by the time a new medium tank was ready to go into full-scale production the weight limit had been upped very considerably.

DEVELOPMENT OF THE SHERMAN

In terms of technology, the American medium tank programme owed much to the vehicles in the 12.2-tonne (12-ton) class with which the British had finished the war, notably the Medium Tank Mark A, known as the 'Whippet', yet the role American policy-makers envisaged for their tanks – infantry support – was very different to the breakthrough role the British mediums had been built to play. The physical requirements of the two types were very much at odds: the infantry support tank needed to by heavily armoured and armed, and had no need of high speed or great endurance. The cavalry or breakthrough tank needed speed and range,

Below: The three Christie-designed track-or-wheel Medium T3 tanks supplied to the US Army at Fort Benning in late 1931 – 'Tornado', 'Hurricane' and 'Cylcone' – seen here running on their wheels.

Above: Delivered in early 1941 and used only for training purposes, the Medium Tank M2A1s had a crew of six, and no less than eight machine guns as well as a short-barrelled 37mm cannon.

and could sacrifice armour and armament to achieve that. On the surface, there seems to have been a basic lack of understanding or perhaps a confusion of aims in the American tank development programme, such as it was, in the 1920s, and it was to go in two quite separate directions, one after the other, as we shall see.

To start with, a pair of prototype vehicles, the M1921 and M1922, were built at Rock Island, the second incorporating the flexible track/cable suspension system devised by a British designer named Philip Johnson, and incorporated into the British Medium Mark D prototype, designed to give high-speed, cross-country performance. They were succeeded in 1924 by the T1, a development of the first prototype with a 200bhp Packard petrol engine, which gave an off-road top speed of 22.5kmh (14mph), and which was standardised for production as the Medium Tank M1 in 1928 but cancelled before manufacture could begin. The sole T1 was used as a testbed for, amongst other things, a 338bhp Liberty engine, and that powerplant was adopted for its successor, the 14.2-tonne (13.9-ton) T2, completed in 1930.

And then came J Walter Christie. Actually, Christie had been around for a while already. He believed that the problems of reliability which had plagued the tanks of World War I could be at least ameliorated if they could run without tracks wherever and whenever possible, and he designed accordingly. The alternative was simpler: utilise trucks and trailers to carry the tanks up to the battlefield assembly area; but Christie rejected this solution, and single-handedly set off to lead tank design down a false trail, though his wider theories were to have far-reaching consequences. He had some justification, for trucks capable of carrying the heavy- and even the medium tanks of the day did not exist, and to have used them would have meant first inventing them. With hindsight, that was the way to go, and so it proved.

To be practical, Christie's track-or-wheel tanks had to be light, and his first attempt, the M1919, weighed 12.2 tonnes (12 tons), dry and unladen. It had four unsprung, rubber-tyred dual roadwheels, one at each corner, and a coil-sprung bogie with a pair of small wheels and a track return roller mounted midway between them on each side. These bogies could be raised and lowered. When the vehicle was in wheel mode, they were lifted clear of the ground; when the 380mm (15in) -wide tracks were fitted they were wound down, and the four roadwheels were lifted clear of the ground instead. Despite the name of Christie's company (the Front Drive Motor Co; he changed it later to the US Wheel Track Layer Corporation), the M1919 was driven from the rear, by engaging teeth on the inside of each track shoe in slots in the spacers between the rear wheel pairs. A 120bhp petrol engine of Christie's own design gave it a maximum speed on its wheels of 21kmh (13mph), and just half that on its tracks, and a fuel capacity of 223l (49 Imp gal/59 US gal) gave it a range of 120km (75 miles) and 55km (35 miles) respectively. It was armed with a 57mm gun with a co-axially mounted .30in machine gun in a round turret, which was surmounted by a round, dome-topped cupola wherein was located another machine gun. It was crewed by three men who were protected by plate a maximum of 25mm (1in) and a minimum of 6.25mm (.25in) thick. Christie withdrew the tank from its trials on 21 April and rebuilt it extensively over the next year, but it was still a long way short of practical. Manoeuvrability was poor and it was mechanically unreliable; it was consigned to the Museum at the US Army's Aberdeen Proving Grounds on 10 July 1924.

RADICAL NEW DESIGNS

Funded by the sale of some patent rights to the US Government, Christie then concentrated on a completely new vehicle which was to have a profound effect on tank design worldwide. In place of the roadwheels and single bogies, the new design, which he called the M1928, had four dual roadwheels per side, each independently sprung and mounted on a pivoted arm which gave a vertical movement of 280mm (11in), with a drive sprocket at the rear and an idler at the front. Power was transmitted to the rear roadwheels by means of a chain from the drive sprocket when the tank was in wheel mode, and the changeover could be accomplished by a trained crew in under 30 minutes. Steering in wheel mode was conventional, and when the change to tracks was effected the front wheels were locked in the fore-and-aft position and the tank was steered by a clutch/brake system, as were all other tracked vehicles of the day. A Liberty engine gave the 8.73-tonne (8.6-ton) vehicle a power-to-weight ratio of 39bhp/ton and a top speed of 112kmh (70mph) on wheels and 67kmh (42mph) on tracks.

After some considerable wrangling, Christie was asked to supply one vehicle, now known as the M1931, to the US Army, and that resulted in a contract for seven examples of the Convertible Medium Tank, T3, which were delivered over the winter of 1931-32. Three of them, with a 37mm gun and a .30in machine gun in their all-round traverse turrets, were assigned to the infantry at Fort Benning, the other four (redesignated as Combat Car, T1, to get around the legal requirement that all tanks had to be allocated to the infantry), with a .50in machine gun in place of the 37mm gun, going to the cavalry at Fort Knox. The tanks had a crew of just two – driver and gunner (an essentially unsatisfactory

Below: The British Army removed the commander's cupola from many of its M3 General Lee tanks. This is an early vehicle – note the M2 gun, with its counterbalance weight at the muzzle – still in service against the Japanese in Burma, in 1944.

arrangement, but one which had been partially validated during World War I in the FT17s) and a top speed limited to 64kmh (40mph) and 40kmh (25mph). The Ordnance Department was not entirely happy with them, and produced a revised specification; Christie argued interminably, and as a result a contract for five additional T3s, with 435bhp Curtiss D-12 aero engines, went not to him but elsewhere; when the T3 was finally superseded by the T4, the last Christie-system American tank, it was built at the Rock Island Arsenal.

Christie did build two more M1931s, which he sold to the Soviet Union; there the suspension system (though little else) was copied for the *Bistrokhodny* Tank (fast tank) series and used virtually unchanged, and was then further developed for the T-34, the tank which was to share the brunt, with the M4 Sherman, of the fighting in the war to come. His suspension system was also used by Poland, in the short-lived 10TP, and by the United Kingdom for a series of cruiser tanks culminating in the A27M Cromwell, the best all-round British tank of World War II, and in modified form, with track return rollers, for the A34 Comet which stayed in service until 1958 and was known, even then, for being faster and more agile across open country than its crews could happily endure. As time went on, Christie's ideas became progressively less orthodox, culminating in his plans for flying tanks fitted with demountable wings.

Above: The Medium Tank, M3, gave the British in North Africa the means to knock out German PzKpfw IVs. It was also the foreruner of the Medium Tank, M4 Sherman.

Sixteen T4s were built in 1935-36; they retained the suspension system of the T3 but were much improved by the addition of a controlled differential steering system along with an air-cooled, radial Continental engine rated at 268bhp which gave a power-to-weight ratio of 19.8bhp/ton and a top speed comparable to that of the original T3. The tank's interior was divided into the now-standard three compartments, with the engine in the rear, the commander and gunner in the turret (along with one .50in and one .30in machine gun), and the driver and a second gunner, with a flexibly mounted .30in machine gun, in the bow. (The use of marine terminology stems from the original British tank development programme, which was instigated by Winston Churchill when he controlled the Royal Navy, as does the name 'tank' itself – that was a subterfuge, designed to maintain secrecy; the original vehicles were described as self-propelled water tanks). Three more tanks, with a fixed barbette in place of the turret and three additional machine guns at the sides and rear, were built as the T4E1. While not particularly significant themselves, they had one important feature which was to influence future American tank design: the barbette extended out to the full width of the tank, above the return run of the track. This was carried forward into the models which evolved from the T4. Both turret and barbette tanks were recommended for standardisation on 6 February

1936, but were turned down by the Adjutant General on the very valid grounds that they had less offensive power than the Light Tank, M2, and cost twice as much to build!

Development of the Medium Tank, T5, was authorised by the Ordnance Committee on 21 May 1936, and thus began the programme which was to lead to the Medium Tank, M4, five years later. When the T5 appeared, it was almost as if Christie had not existed. Gone were the large roadwheels, together with the dual track-or-wheel transmission, and instead the tank had three two-wheeled bogies with vertical volute springs, with track return rollers located between them; the drive was via a multi-plate clutch and a long transmission shaft to the constant-mesh five forward/one reverse gearbox at the front of the vehicle, the sprockets and the idlers having changed places (an intrinsically less satisfactory situation, actually, for it places the track return run under tension; it was introduced to simplify the installation of controlled differential steering). The engine used in the T4 was retained, even though there had been some criticism of its power output and the all-up weight had increased to slightly over 15.24 tonnes (15 tons). Nonetheless, there was

16bhp/ton available, and that gave the T5 a maximum speed, on the road, of slightly over 50kmh (30mph).

In terms of deployment, infantry support was the constant theme running through the US medium tank development programme (and had been the *raison d'être* for assigning all the tanks to the infantry in the first place) and the T5's armament – if not its level of protection – reflected that, for it had a 37mm gun in a fully traversing turret (in fact, the Phase I tanks as completed had a pair of relatively low velocity 37mm M2A1 guns, the mount for a new version, the M3, having been delayed) which was set atop a covered barbette with flexibly mounted .30in machine guns in sponsons at each corner and two more in the front plate, where they were accessible to the driver. Multiple machine gun installations require extra hands to man them, and the T5 had a crew of five – a commander, driver and three gunners. Protection was certainly inadequate, even by the meagre standards of the day, with a maximum of 25mm (1in) and a minimum of 6.25mm (.25in) of plate; this was improved significantly in the Phase III version (there were no Phase II tanks) when the weight limit was upped to more than 20.3 tonnes (20 tons).

The T5 Phase I was recommended for standardisation as the Medium Tank, M2, on 2 June 1938, and approved, but development continued even as production tooling was assembled – the armour was thickened to a maximum of 37mm (one and a half inches) in the turret and 32mm (1.25in) in the hull, and the Continental engine was replaced by a nine-cylinder Wright air-cooled radial with a nominal output of 400bhp (though those tested actually developed only 345bhp). Top speed climbed to almost 53kmh (33mph), but fuel consumption increased, and reduced the maximum range to 160km (100 miles) despite the capacity having been increased to 505l (111 Imp gal/133 US gal). A 400bhp Guiberson air-cooled radial diesel engine was fitted to one Phase III tank (and the experiment was continued briefly, and eventually fruitlessly, in the M3 in 1941 and in the M4 in 1943-44), and another was (extensively) modified to take a 75mm M1A1 howitzer in place of the forward/right machine gun sponson, the 37mm gun in the turret being replaced by

Below: A beautifully restored M4A1 Sherman, distinguished by its cast upper hull. This model was the first Sherman to come off the production lines, starting in February 1942.

a machine gun. Clearly, the development of the Medium Tank M3 owed something to this prototype, which was known as the T5E2.

The Medium Tank, M2, went into production in the summer of 1939 at the Rock Island Arsenal. With plate somewhat heavier than that of the T5 Phase I and an improved powerplant, it had a power-to-weight ratio of 18.4bhp/ton, and 337mm- (13.25in) wide tracks gave it a zero-penetration ground pressure of 1.32kg/sq cm (18.8psi) when fully loaded. The suspension was modified slightly, the track return rollers now located in the bogies instead of between them. The number of machine guns was increased by two to eight (the extras were located in the roof of the barbette, to combat air attack), and the crew went up to six. Just 18 vehicles were authorised for production in the first fiscal year, and a further 54 were to have been funded from the budget for the following year. But as production got underway, events in Europe indicated the design was already obsolete . . .

Even as the M2s were coming off the line, the specification was being hastily modified, and the M2A1 replaced it. It had vertical sides to its turret to increase the room inside; the armour of the T5 Phase III; a somewhat more powerful Wright R975 EC2 engine and tracks widened by 25mm (one inch) to reduce the ground pressure to 1.08kg/sq cm (15.3psi). Hydraulic power steering made the driver's task considerably easier.

THE US PREPARES FOR WAR

And then, in May 1940, Hitler demonstrated that the lightning war he had waged on Poland the previous September had been anything but a flash in the pan as he turned his armies west to over-run the Low Countries and France, and informed opinion in the United States military establishment began to consider very seriously the probability of having to go to war sooner rather than later. On 10 July a separate tank command, the Armored Force, came back into being under Major-General Adna Chaffee, with a nominal strength of two divisions and one separate battalion, but actually able to field just 18 modern tanks – the M1s produced the previous year. And neither they nor the M2A1s which were even then in the pilot production stage at Rock Island were any match for *Panzerkampfwagen* IVs, with 75mm guns capable of penetrating the American armour from well outside stand-off range. Nonetheless – and almost unbelievably – negotiations between William Knudsen, lately head of General Motors but now in charge of US military production, and K.T. Keller, head of the Chrysler Corporation, led to a contract for Chrysler to produce 1000 M2A1 tanks in two years. It was signed on 15 August 1940, and cancelled, after Chaffee intervened, just 13 days later, to be replaced by a similar deal to produce 1000 M3s – essentially M2A1s with a sponson-mounted 75mm gun, similar to the experimental installation in the T5E2 – which had been standardised the day after

Chaffee took command. In the end, 94 M2A1 tanks were actually delivered, and were used for training purposes.

Initially the new tank was to have had a full complement of machine guns, but a re-think of the likely tactical requirements followed, and eliminated those mounted in sponsons; instead, the turret would carry a high-velocity 37mm M3 gun and a co-axially-mounted .30in machine gun, and a superimposed cupola would carry an anti-aircraft machine gun. (The British, who were major users of the M3 tank, deleted the cupola from some of their vehicles and fitted them with bigger turrets, calling them the 'General Grant'. The original design, with cupola, was known in British service as the 'General Lee', but, confusingly, some had the cupola removed; the sure way to tell a Grant from a Lee was by the presence, in the former, of a distinct overhang in the turret sides and rear, which latter almost amounts to a bustle.)

The Medium Tank, M3, which first saw action on 27 May 1942, deserves a study of its own, and certainly made a major contribution to the winning of World War II if only because it gave the British armoured divisions in North Africa the means to kill PzKpfw IVs predictably, and was thus instrumental in preventing Rommel's *Deutsches Afrika Korps* from winning through to the Suez Canal and beyond, but for our purposes, we can see it simply as the direct forerunner of the Medium Tank, M4 Sherman.

The tank's major deficiency lay in its main armament. The characteristics of the 75mm M2 gun, which had started life as the unsuccessful T6 low-velocity anti-aircraft gun (which in turn had been developed from the French M1897 *soixante-quinze* field gun, as fitted to the first French tanks, the Schneider and St. Chamond), were actually adequate enough, both in the point and area-fire roles, as its selection to go forward (in its slightly longer, M3 form) into the first versions of the M4 was to prove; its armour-piercing, capped, ballistic-capped (APCBC) rounds were capable of penetrating over 50mm (two inches) of homogeneous armour at a 30 degree angle at 900m (985yds) range, and it could reach out to 10km (10,940yds) with its high-explosive (HE) shells. But the siting of the gun – in a sponson, with just 30 degrees of independent movement – put its crews at a distinct tactical disadvantage.

This shortcoming was understood from the start, but (and it is worth bearing in mind that Hitler's declaration of war on the United States was still some months away, and that there was a strong – though not over-riding – popular sentiment in the USA for abstention from what was seen as a purely European affair) so was the imperative to begin production of the best tanks available, in significant numbers, at the earliest possible moment. As a result, substantial contracts for M3 production were signed, and 6258 were manufactured, in six different versions, between June 1941 and December 1942. But even while the ink on the first of them was still wet, Chaffee's Armored Force submitted detailed characteristics for a tank to replace it.

CHAPTER 2

Design and Development of the M4 Sherman

The initial design for the M4 Sherman was drawn up in 1941, and its initial layout was defined two years earlier, but the tank was to go through many stages of development before the final examples rolled out of the factories in mid-1945.

When the outline specification for the new American medium tank was drawn up, the emphasis was firmly on capitalising on the (admittedly, as yet untested) strengths of the M3, and incorporating as many components from it as possible into the new design. It was never intended to be a new, from-the-ground-up creation, but was, rather, a further stage in the evolutionary process which had effectively begun with the T5/Medium Tank, M2. Though the decision in principle to develop a new tank had been taken on the last day of the previous August, it was 18 April 1941 before the necessary planning conference was held at the Aberdeen Proving Grounds, since all the available armoured fighting vehicle design staff had been occupied throughout the intervening autumn and winter in getting out the finalised production drawings for the M3. At that meeting it was decided to retain the basic chassis of the M3, including the lower hull, suspension, transmission and powerplant. Happily, the lower hull had been designed around the Wright R975 EC2, and the engine bay was big enough to accommodate more powerful powerplants with very different configurations (though not without difficulty), and this was to be significant in the future. The upper hull would also use as many M3 components as possible, while the tank's fighting furniture would also remain the same for the most part (and for the moment), though it would be arranged very differently.

Left: Late-model M4A1s of the Israeli Defence Force, equipped with 76mm guns and with one-piece cast differential covers, which mark them as having been manufactured in 1944 or 1945, in parade order prior to the withdrawal from Sinai in December 1956.

The reason for the M3's main gun being sponson-mounted was simply that there was not, in the United States, a turret big enough to bear its 355kg (782lb) weight (the 75mm gun M3 specified for the new tank was 50kg (110lb) heavier still, being somewhat longer in the barrel), and the design of that essential component was the first priority. It was to be basically similar to the turret of the M3, being a squat cylinder with a flattened, angled front face (but with that angle brought nearer to the vertical), and with a bustle added at the rear to house the radio set. It was based on a 1753mm (69in) diameter ring (that of the M3 was 1384mm [54.5in]), and like its smaller predecessor, would have power traverse and gyroscopically controlled stabilisation in elevation. With the benefit of hindsight, it is clear that it should have been bigger from the start, to have allowed heavier armament to have been fitted; as it was, the up-gunning process had to wait for a new design (based on the same turret ring dimensions), proposed for the T20-series tanks. The turret was to have a removable front plate or mantlet, to allow a variety of different types of alternative armaments to be fitted, and early on the possibilities were established to be: a 75mm L/40.1 M3 gun with a co-axial .30in machine gun (an M2 gun was to be substituted in the pilot and very early production models, while the mount for the bigger gun was developed); two 37mm L/56.6 M6 guns with a .30in machine gun; three .50in machine guns, mounted at a high angle; one six-pounder L/52.1 Mark V gun (a British high-velocity anti-tank gun with

adequate performance but a low projectile weight) with a co-axial .30in machine gun or one 105mm M2A1 howitzer with a .30in machine gun. Eventually, as we shall see, Sherman tanks were to be armed with an even greater variety of weapons, though only two of those original combinations ever saw the light of day. In addition, the turret was to have the superimposed commander's cupola from the M3, with its high-angle .30in anti-aircraft machine gun, and the two forward-firing, driver-operated .30in machine guns (which could be elevated or depressed from +8 to -6 degrees and locked off there) mounted in the front plate alongside the flexibly-mounted .30in machine gun, were also to be retained (they were deleted in March of the following year, having been found to be little more than a distracting hindrance).

Apart from the basic tactical advantage conveyed by all-round traversability, placing the main armament in the turret (and thereby deleting a gun – the 37mm) allowed the crew to be cut to five: driver (on the left) and assistant driver/bow gunner in the front compartment, separated by the transmission; gunner (to the right of the gun), loader (to its left) and commander (behind the gunner) in the turret. This arrangement was to be the standard in US tanks until the introduc-

Below: A restored M4A1(76)W HVSS. Note the lack of sandshields covering the track return run, the 585mm (23in) tracks and the revised bogies. Almost 3500 models were produced in the last 18 months of the war.

Above: An early M4 Sherman – note the bolted, three-piece transmission cover – detraining from a flat car via an end-ramp. Some 6748 of these 75mm gun tanks were produced between July 1942 and January 1944.

tion of the M41 Walker Bulldog and M48 Patton in 1952, wherein the flexibly mounted bow gun was deleted and never to be reinstated. Removing the sponson also simplified the hull form and eliminated some very nasty potential shot-traps, lowered the profile – the M3 measured 3125mm (123in) to the top of its cupola; the prototype M4 was 203mm (eight inches) lower and the first production variant, with the cupola deleted, was 152mm (six inches) lower still – and reduced the surface area of armour, allowing that which remained to be thicker without increasing the vehicle's all-up weight. As originally specified, the other dimensions of the tank were exactly the same as those of the M3, of course – a length of 5639mm (222in) and a width of 2718mm (107in) – but these were to be modified before the production run started, and the M4 was 254mm (10in) longer and 100mm (four inches) narrower. Some subsequent versions were lengthened, and when a new suspension system was introduced the overall width increased.

REFINING THE DESIGN

A full-size wooden mock-up was constructed in May, approved by the Ordnance Committee the following month, and the new vehicle was designated the Medium Tank, T6. Aberdeen was then ordered to begin work on a pilot tank with an upper hull cast in one piece, while the Rock Island Arsenal was to start work on another, with its upper hull

fabricated from sheets of rolled homogeneous steel welded together to the same basic form. The Aberdeen pilot was completed on 2 September, with a short M2 gun (which had to be fitted with a counter-weight at the muzzle, giving it a somewhat odd appearance, so that the elevation gyro-stabil-isation system, as fitted to the 37mm gun in the M3, could be tested). It seems that the commander's cupola was never fitted, though the turret was equipped to receive it.

Clearly, the design conformed to the outline plan very well, for there were just three quite minor modifications made before it was ordered into production, and two of them related to access: hatches in the upper hull sides above the track run, which gave onto the interior via the sponsons, were deleted, which both improved the integrity of the armour and increased the available internal storage space; and a hatch, a mirror-image of that located over the driver's head, was introduced for the bow gunner. (There was no hatch save for the command position in the original turret; one was added for the loader, beside the commander's hatch, just before half-way through the production run of the M4A2 in January 1944, and kits were produced which allowed the modification to be retro-fitted to earlier tanks.) A similar

fitting was included as original equipment in the enlarged turret developed for the still-born T23 tank and fitted to the Sherman to allow the mounting of the 76mm M1 gun after the attempt to get it into the original turret had failed, and was also introduced into the turret of the British Firefly (see below). There was an escape hatch in the floor, positioned close behind the assistant driver's seat, but of course this was never used under normal conditions. The commander's cupola was eliminated from the production turret, too, and the hatch combing raised, a two-part hatch cover installed and a high-angle mounting for a machine gun fitted instead. An order of 5 September standardised the new vehicle as the Medium Tank, M4, and another of 11 December differentiated between the two sub-types, the tanks with welded upper hulls being designated as the Medium Tank, M4, and those with cast upper hulls becoming M4A1s. Both types had identical cast homogeneous steel turrets. The M4 had a slightly greater internal volume, allowing the storage of a few extra 75mm rounds - 97, in place of the M4A1's 90.

THE ARMOUR

In terms of the thickness of the armour, there was no difference between the welded hulls and the cast, though the rounded form of the M4A1 may have been slightly more effective when it came to deflecting incoming rounds. The angles at which the armour was set did vary somewhat, and in theory this altered one or the other tank's ultimate vulner-

Above: An M4A2 of the Essex Yeomanry at speed in France in the late summer of 1944. This is a troop commander's tank – note the radio antenna on the mounting on the forward glacis, adjacent to the bow gunner.

ability – but in practice the difference was minimal. There are no hard-and-fast rules regarding the effectiveness of angled armour, since so much depends on the attitude of the entire vehicle *vis-à-vis* its opponent. By the time the Sherman appeared, it was generally seen as essential to encourage the deflection of incoming rounds – a notion with a certain optimistic attraction to it, but one which was not entirely borne out in practice and depended very much on the angle of attack – and to increase the effective thickness of the plate. In terms of simple geometry, armour set at a 30 degree angle can be 20 per cent thinner – and therefore, lighter – than vertical armour, and still provide the same level of protection, but there is also the matter of internal volume to be considered. The German PzKpfw VI Tiger, a contemporary of the Sherman and the last major 'square' tank, made little use of angled armour and relied on extra-thick plate instead; it was very much overweight, and was a less effective tank than it might have been as a result.

Only once in the entire production run was the angle of the Sherman's armour modified; late in the run of M4A2 tanks, in the spring of 1944, the (welded) glacis plate of the upper hull of that type was brought closer to the vertical, to

VEHICLE DESIGNATIONS

In American service, all M4-series tanks were known as 'General Shermans' and the types were differentiated by the A-suffix – thus, from M4A1 to M4A6 (though there was no -A5; that designation was used for the M3 Medium-derived Ram tank built in Canada). The ruling difference was in the powerplants, and only two types, the M4A4 and the short-lived M4A6, shared a different hull, and then it was simply lengthened to accommodate their bigger engines. Sub-types were sometimes distinguished by the addition of an E-suffix, of the calibre of the main gun in millimetres (in brackets), of 'W', to indicate wet stowage of main gun ammunition, and of 'HVSS' (or -E8) for tanks with horizontal volute spring suspension and the wide tracks which went with it; thus, the M4A3(76)W HVSS was an M4A3 with the Ford V-8 engine common to all its type, with the 76mm gun, wet ammunition stowage and horizontal volute spring suspension. The sheer variety of Shermans produced means that the designation system is not absolutely transparent, though each designation was unique. The British, who were to be the first to go into battle with them, gave their Shermans Roman-numeral sub-type designators; the M4 was to become the Sherman I and the M4A1 the Sherman II, for example. They later appended a capital-letter, gun-type designator – 'A' for the 76mm gun; 'B' for the 105mm M4 howitzer; and 'C' for the high-velocity 17-pounder gun which the Americans never took up (tanks armed with which they also called the 'Firefly'). They added 'Y' where the Americans used HVSS and prefixed the whole name with 'Hybrid' to distinguish tanks with the cast-and-welded upper hull introduced later. (See the appendix on page 94 for a complete breakdown of production statistics.) The British style of designation leads to some straightforward difficulties of interpretation: 'Sherman VC' should be read as 'Sherman Five C', not 'Vee Cee' and Sherman IVY – the British designation of the M4A3(76)W HVSS – should be read as 'Sherman Four Y', not 'Ivy', though that scarcely presents a problem save in theory, for there were only seven M4A3s supplied to the British Army.

It was the British, who were used to naming their weapons and vehicles, rather than just designating them with letters and numbers, who began the practice of giving American tanks the names of distinguished American cavalry-men, starting with J.E.B. Stuart, after whom they named the M3 (and M5) light tanks and continuing with Ulysses S. Grant and Robert E. Lee, after whom the M3 medium tank variants were named. It was they who named the M4 Medium after William Tecumseh Sherman, and the Americans followed suit, later adopting the practice for themselves, and the M26 Pershing, the M24 Chaffee, the M41 Walker Bulldog, the M46, M47 and M48 Patton, the M551 Sheridan and the M1 Abrams were all thus named from their standardisation. (Walker wasn't a cavalryman, though he had commanded armoured brigades, divisions and corps; he was commander of ground forces in Korea. It had been the intention to name the M41 the 'Little Bulldog', but the designation was changed to honour Walker, who was killed in a motor accident; he was small of stature and renowned for his 'pugnacious tenacity' – qualities with which its designers' hoped they had endowed the diminutive M41.)

47 degrees instead of 56 degrees as the original design had specified, and the plate was thickened by 12.7mm (.5in), to compensate for the change. This allowed the fairing necessary to accommodate the hatches for the crewmen in the front compartment to be eliminated (while the hatches themselves were actually increased in size), which meant that the glacis plate could now be a single sheet of rolled steel without a welded joint and with considerably greater integrity as a result. The geometry of cast hulls was never modified in this way.

The upper and lower portions of the front of the Sherman's hull were protected to 50mm (2in), the sides and rear to 37mm (1.5in), the deck to between 12.7mm and 18.75mm (.5in to .75in) and the floor to 25mm (1in) in front and 12.7mm (.5in) in the rear. The turret front was 75mm (3in) thick, and a 50mm- (2in) thick rotor shield attached to the gun tube, which protected the slot in which the gun elevated and depressed, was added soon after production

began), the sides and rear 50mm (2in) and the top, 25mm (1in). Some of these dimensions were increased, though not enormously, in some later models, as we shall see, but there is no doubt that compared to some of the German tanks it was to encounter, the Sherman was only lightly protected. There were to be many instances of German high-velocity 8.8cm and 7.5cm armour-piercing rounds passing right through the tank, penetrating the two layers of armour cleanly. German doctrine had it that a PzKpfw V Panther, with the 7.5cm KwK42 gun, could destroy a Sherman head-on at 1000m (1100yds), and from the side or rear at 2800m (3060yds) – roughly twice the distance, in each case, than those at which the Sherman could destroy the Panther, which was an overwhelming advantage – at least in theory. The figures for the heavier Tiger tank, with its thicker armour and more powerful 8.8cm gun, were even more impressive (or depressing, depending on which side one happened to find one's self).

Late-model M4A2

0.7m (28in)

3.73m (12.25ft)

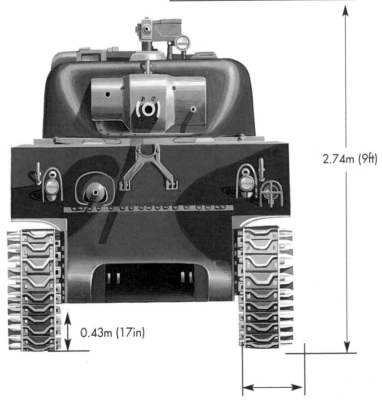

2.74m (9ft)

0.43m (17in)

0.61m (24in) including extenders

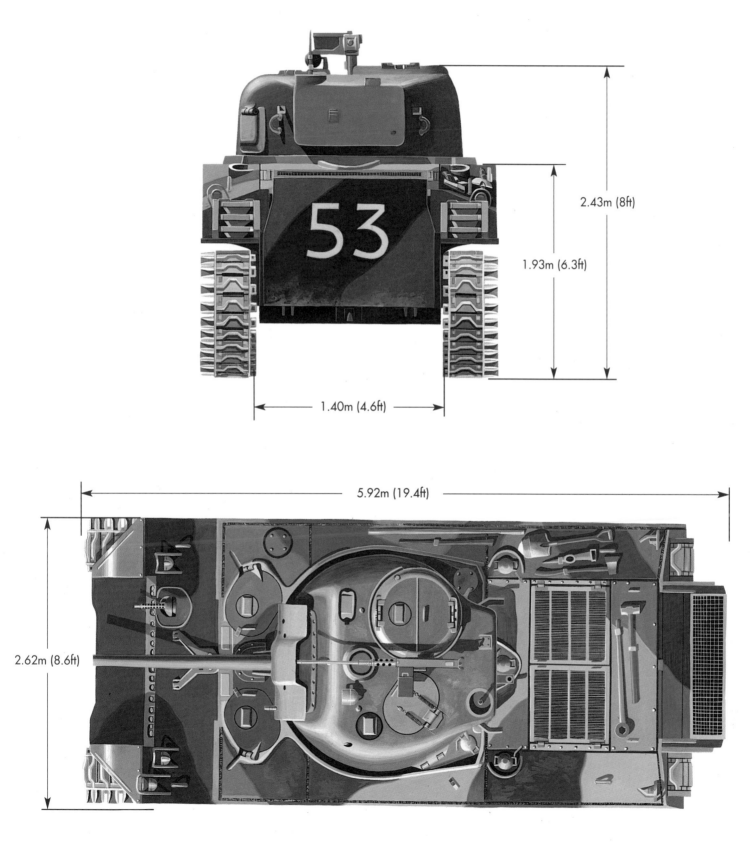

2.43m (8ft)

1.93m (6.3ft)

1.40m (4.6ft)

5.92m (19.4ft)

2.62m (8.6ft)

The 'blueprint' weights of the initial versions of the tank, when fitted with the M3 gun in the M34A1 mount – the standard for production vehicles of these types – were almost identical (the cast hull was some 45kg (100lb) lighter at just under 30.45 tonnes (29.9 tons) with a combat load of fuel and ammunition, and that was an increase of almost 3.2 tonnes (3.1 tons) over the weight of the prototype T6. Other types introduced later varied somewhat; the heaviest 'normal' gun tank was the M4A2(76)W (that is, with the 76mm M1 cannon in the M62 mount, and wet ammunition stowage) at 33.30 tonnes (32.77 tons). The heaviest Sherman of all, the extensively up-armoured M4A3E2 Assault Tank, with its much thicker frontal and turret protection, which was manufactured only in small numbers (see Chapter 4), weighed 38.2 tonnes (37.5 tons).

POWERPLANTS AND VEHICLE TYPES

The nine-cylinder R975 (its designation was an approximation of its capacity in cubic inches) radial engine fitted to all the M4 and M4A1 tanks, identical to that fitted to the first M3s, did much to define the form the entire Sherman range would take. Developed originally by Wright, its manufacture and subsequent modification were taken over by Continental. It was mounted in the rear of the vehicle with its shaft inclined at 10 degrees from the horizontal, the drive shaft running forward and down, below the turret floor, to the transmission and final drive at the front. By the time the ancillaries were fitted, the powerplant was virtually 'square' (that is, its width, and height, were the same as its overall length), and as a result it was possible to fit the other powerplants employed in the Sherman-series tanks – the Ford GAA V-8 and the idiosyncratic Chrysler A57 'multi-bank' engine as well as the siamese-twin GM 6046 12-cylinder diesel – into the same space, by the relatively straightforward operation of increasing the tank's overall length slightly where necessary. The use of different engines was simplified by the powerplant and gearbox being separated. Ignition in the Wright engine was by means of a magneto, and the petrol/air mixture was fed to the cylinders under pressure from a supercharger. All M4-series tanks were fitted with a small single-cylinder two-stroke auxiliary motor which drove a second generator set, allowing electrical systems to be powered-up while the main powerplant was switched off without depleting the batteries (this was particularly significant for the turret traverse system, of course, and meant that the tank didn't need its main engine running in order to be able to fight; thus, it could lie quietly in ambush).

M4A1 PRODUCTION

The M4A1 went into production much earlier than the M4; in fact, the M4A2 was the first welded-hull tank to go into series manufacture in April 1942. The British Government's Tank Mission, headed by Michael Dewar and including an experienced designer of armoured vehicles, L.E. Carr (it was

Above: American infantrymen enjoy the protection of an M4A3 tank, just after the D-Day landings. Note the Rhinoceros device on the bow, and the appliqué armour panels on the sponson side and the turret.

Right: Later-model M4 Shermans, with cast, one-piece transmission covers but still with the all-welded hulls, wait in the loading bay of the Detroit Tank Arsenal.

he who designed the bigger turret for the British 'General Grant' M3s), and Major-General Douglas Pratt, who had commanded the British tanks at Arras in France just months before, and who probably knew as much about actually fighting them in the field as anyone on the Allied side then on active service, had arrived in Washington, DC, in the late summer of 1940 – the UK's blackest hour following the disaster in France and the hurried evacuation of the British Army from Dunkirk – when the M3 was just going into production. Dewar ordered 3000 M3s (which was more than double the number for which he had received authorisation), 'spending' all the British Government's investments in the United States, which totalled $240 million, in the process, but he included in the contract a provision to shift half the order over to any better medium tank which might go into production, and very promptly opted for the M4 as soon as it was mooted. As luck should have it, one of the would-be manufacturers of the M3s for Britain, the Lima Locomotive Co, was late in establishing its production line; it was switched over to Shermans instead and came on stream very quickly as a result. The first Lima-produced M4A1s were

M4 PRODUCTION

Production of the M4 started up at the Pressed Steel Car Co plant in July, 1942, and ceased there in August 1943; it was taken up at the Baldwin Locomotive Works from January 1943 to January 1944; at ALCO (the American Locomotive Co) from February to December 1943; at the Pullman Standard Car Co between May and September 1943 and at the Chrysler-run Detroit Tank Arsenal from August 1943 to January 1944. Between them, these five manufacturers produced a total of 6748 M4s, a little over 13.5 per cent of the total. A further 1641 were completed with the 105mm M4 howitzer between February 1944 and March 1945. The later M4s produced at the Detroit Tank Arsenal were actually something of a hybrid of the two early types, in that the whole of the upper hull front, as far back as the driver's and bow gunner's hatches, was a single-piece casting, which was welded to the rolled homogeneous plate which made up the rest of the unit.

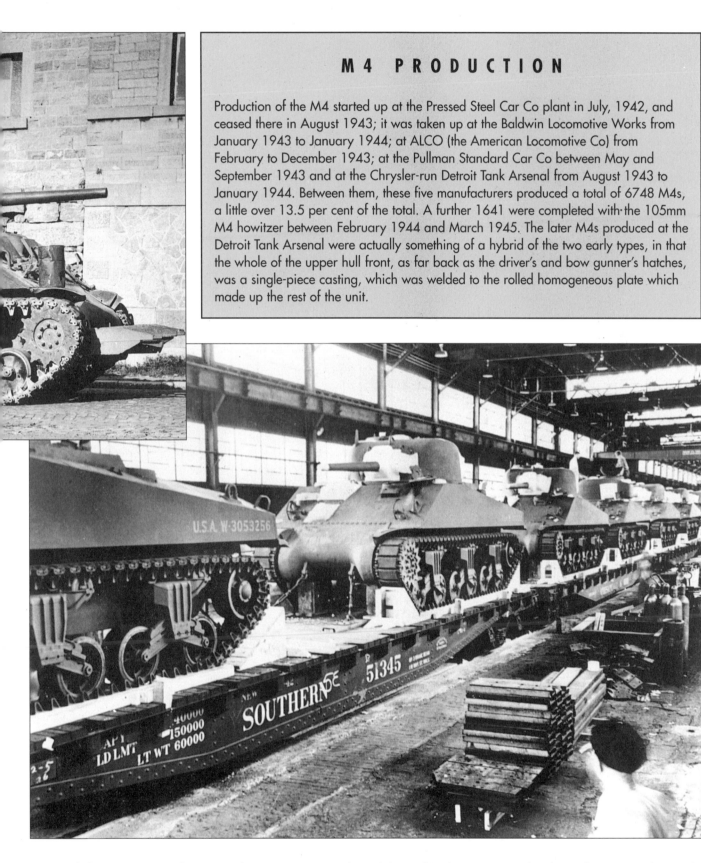

accepted for service in February, 1942; it was six months more before the first M4s were delivered.

Production of the M4A1 also got underway elsewhere, at the Pressed Steel Car Co in March 1942 (car manufacturers had been brought into the tank production programme with the M3; Chrysler was the major builder of that tank, having delivered its first on 21 April 1941) and, in May, at the Pacific Car and Foundry Co. Lima ceased production in September 1942, Pacific Car and Foundry Co stopped in November, and Pressed Steel Car Co followed the next month. Between them, they were to build 6281 M4A1s, almost 12.5 per cent of the total of 49,234 Sherman gun-tanks completed. A further 3426 M4A1s were completed with the 76.2mm M1 high-velocity cannon and wet ammunition storage as M4A1(76)Ws, between January 1944 and July 1945.

EARLY MODIFICATIONS

This was not the only modification made during the 23-month production run of the M4 and M4A1. Some were minor, and made to simplify production as much as anything, or to make it cheaper; some were made to improve the tank's performance or correct a shortcoming which had been overlooked in the original design or specification, but others came about as a response to weaknesses turned up in extended training and in combat. Not all the modifications listed were made to M4s and M4A1s before the later types of Sherman were introduced, and thus we find early-production M4A2s and -A3s (for example) finished to an earlier specification. Likewise, some modifications were retro-fitted, either in the field or when damaged but salvageable tanks or those used in training were 're-manufactured', either as gun-tanks or as one of the many specialist variants.

Perhaps the most significant changes were made to the early models' powerplant and the suspension system, while the most obvious concerned the structure of the very front of the vehicle and the fitting of sand shields. The R975 EC2 engine was soon superseded by the similar R975 C1, also of 15,937cc (973 cu. in) but with its compression ratio reduced from 6.3:1 to 5.7:1, which reduced the necessary octane rating of the fuel from 92 to 80. Other improvements had actually raised the net power output by 10 brake horse-power to 350bhp, which meant that performance was essentially unchanged. Experience showed that the six pairs of heavy 178mm (seven inch) -diameter springs on which the tank rode were not sufficiently strong; they were replaced by springs 203mm (eight inches) in diameter, and the trunnion pin, which linked the two arms of the bogie, was raised. This modification meant that there was no longer space to mount the track return rollers on top of the vertical component of the bogies, and it was moved to the rear and a track skid fitted in its place. The dimensions of the roadwheels remained unchanged at 508mm (20in) in diameter and 230mm (9in) wide. All-steel track shoes were also introduced, alongside the originals which were fitted with rubber pads, chiefly due to the shortage of rubber after the Japanese over-ran Southeast Asia in early 1942 (a single set of tracks required almost three quarters of a ton of rubber!) but also to improve wear and grip in cross-country operation.

The biggest alteration in the tank's appearance came with the substitution of a one-piece casting for the original three-piece fabricated transmission cover which formed the very nose of the tank, with its distinctive twin flanges and bolts.

Below: An early version of the M4 with the 105mm Howitzer, M4. In all, 1641 of these tanks, intended primarily for infantry support, were produced between February 1944 and March 1945.

The new component was both considerably stronger than the original, and improved the alignment of the gear trains in the transmission which it housed. Initially, the new castings were cylindrical, but later a more angular version, which was more effective at deflecting incoming armour-piercing rounds, was produced. It was known as the 'Mary Ann', seemingly because its profile resembled that of a young worker of that name at the Detroit Tank Arsenal, where it was produced. Not all the M4 types got the cast transmission cover; even the last M4A4s, produced in the summer of 1943, still had the three-piece fabrication.

Early production tanks had only very rudimentary mud or sand guards in front of and behind the sponsons, though of course the latter themselves acted as covers for the return track run. Those which arrived in Egypt in time for the Battle of El Alamein, in the autumn of 1942, were mostly without sand shields, which were fabricated and fitted locally. From the summer of 1942, sand shields, which extended around the upper parts of the sprockets and idlers and down to enclose the return track run completely, were fitted to most tanks during manufacture. Many of the tanks which arrived with the American forces in North Africa, after the Operation Torch landings, were also without sand guards. Tanks destined for northern Europe in 1944 and 1945 were finished without sand shields.

The R975 C1 engine was replaced in mid-1943 by the C4 variant, which ran rather cooler thanks to improvements in heat dissipation brought about by modifying the cooling fins to increase their area. A new carburettor and higher charging pressure increased the net power output to 400bhp and improved the torque by 25 per cent, which had a huge effect on the tank's cross-country performance. It had been suggested (by the Ordnance Committee) that a series of modifications to the engine bay, to improve air flow and accessibility, be made to new C4-engined tanks, but other factors made that impossible.

At a dry weight of 555kg (1220lb), the C4 had a gross power-to-weight ratio of almost .83bhp/kg, which compared very favourably indeed with the .71bhp/kg of the Ford GAA V-8, which was reckoned to be the best all-round engine fitted to any of the Shermans (see the M4A3, below). It was also better than the Meteor engine fitted to the British Cromwells, Comets and Centurions (.80bhp/kg) and streets ahead of the Maybach HL230 which powered the German Tigers and Panthers, which gave just .58bhp/kg. (The respective power-to-capacity ratios for those four engines was 34.6, 36, 45 and 30.4 brake horsepower per litre, which seems to tell a different story. The power-to-weight ratios are the more important factor here.) It was considerably more complicated than the Ford unit, however, and was thus both potentially less reliable and more expensive as a result. Nonetheless, R975-series engines in their various forms powered over 18,000 Sherman gun-tanks (and around 5000 M3s, too).

Above: A late version of the 105mm-armed M4. Note the modified gunshield and waterproofing gasket, and especially the horizontal volute spring system (HVSS) and wide tracks.

M4A2

The third Sherman variant, the M4A2 (which the British called the Sherman III) was fitted with a General Motors 'siamese-twin' 12-cylinder two-stroke diesel engine of 13,922cc (850cu. in) capacity, which gave 375bhp net and a top speed of around 48kmh (30mph) – some 20 per cent higher than that of the earlier models. Thanks to the inherent characteristics of the compression-ignition engine, it had good low-speed torque, which equated to good cross-country performance, and as much as 30 per cent better fuel consumption than a petrol engine of similar size. It was held to be somewhat temperamental, however, and was particularly sensitive to dirt. The engine was of somewhat curious construction, being essentially two GM 6-71 truck engines set side-by-side. One of the virtues of this engine was its symmetrical construction; all that was necessary to pair them was to modify the cylinder head arrangement of one of them so that its induction and exhaust were swopped to the other side. Both rotated in the same direction. Each retained its own crankshaft, flywheel and clutch, and could drive the tank on its own if necessary, via a helical gear which meshed with another common to both, which was attached to the propeller shaft. As first produced the engine had dry-sump lubrication and a separate oil tank, but this was altered to the more conventional wet-sump system before production got underway. Its cooling system and air cleaners were modified, too. Due to its form, the drive shaft which connected it to the transmission was much lower down than in the radial-engined tanks, which meant much better clearance beneath the turret basket floor. A total of 8053 75mm-armed and 2915 76mm-armed M4A2 gun-tanks were produced, and the type had the longest continuous production run, being manufactured in its two variants from April 1942 to May 1945, at the Fisher Tank Arsenal and at Pullman initially, and later at ALCO, Baldwin, and the Federal Machine and Welder Co. Following a decision of March 1942, that only petrol-driven tanks would be sent overseas with US combat units, the M4A2s were produced largely for Allied use, though a few were employed in training units. This was the tank shipped in the largest quantities to the Soviet Union, where diesel power was the norm; in all, 1990 M4A2s with the 75mm gun were sent, and 2073 up-gunned M4A2(76)Ws. The United Kingdom got most of the remainder – 5046 in total. Only on two exceptional occasions were American forces to use the diesel-powered M4s: the US 1st Armoured Division which landed in North Africa as part of Operation Torch was equipped with some, and so were units of the US Marine Corps which landed on Okinawa, right at the war's end.

M4A3

Next in sequence came the 18,017cc (1100cu. in) Ford GAA, a liquid-cooled petrol engine with its eight cylinders arranged in a 60 degree vee, which developed 450bhp net. It was two-thirds of a V-12 unit developed as an aero engine,

and was first tested aboard a modified M3 in February 1942. This is widely held to have been the best all-round engine produced for the M4 series, and the basic tank it powered, the M4A3, was the variant the US Army kept for itself (only seven were sent to the USA's allies during World War II, all of them to the UK, where they were known as Sherman IVs. This pattern had nothing to do with the quality of the variants; it made very sound logistical sense to group the tanks' distribution in this way, allowing standardisation of

Right: A late-model M4A1, with the Type Two turret, 76mm M1A1 gun, wet ammunition storage, horizontal volute springs and 585mm- (23in-) wide tracks. A total of 3426 M4A1(76)Ws were produced between January 1944 and July 1945.

Below: Early M4A1 tanks, easily identifiable thanks to the rounded lines of their cast hulls, pictured during training. A total of 6281 75mm-armed M4A1s were produced between February 1942 and December 1943.

maintenance procedures and of spare parts-keeping). The GAA installation was the most accessible of all the Sherman powerplants, and was thus relatively easy to work on. Some 662l (146 Imp gal/175 US gal) of fuel, which was stored in exactly the same way as it had been in the earlier types, with a 273l (60 Imp gal/71 US gal) horizontal tank in each sponson and a 125l (27.5 Imp gal/33 US gal) vertical tank in the front corners of the engine compartment, gave the tank a range of around 210km (130 miles). It could sustain a

maximum speed, on the road, of 42kmh (26mph). In all, 12,342 M4A3s were produced, and it was the only variant manufactured with all three (American) gun types: the 75mm M3, the 76mm M1 and the 105mm M4 howitzer. None were converted to the Firefly configuration (see below).

M4A4

The most peculiar of all the powerplants to grace mass-produced Shermans was surely the Chrysler A57 multi-bank engine, which was composed of no fewer than five six-cylinder units mated to a single drive shaft via a transfer gearbox with a ratio of 1.16:1. In theory, the result was a nightmare, with five distributors, five carburettors, five fuel pumps, five water pumps – five of everything! It was very bulky, too, and the only way to get it in was to extend the tank's hull by 280mm (11in) and eliminate the vertical fuel tanks in the engine bay (the sponson tanks were increased in size to 303l/67 Imp gal/80 US gal each, which went some way

towards compensating, but the M4A4/Sherman V, as the A57-engined tank was known, still had the shortest endurance of any Sherman gun tank as a result) and incorporate bulges into the rear deck and the floor to provide clearance for the cooling fan and the upper part of the radiator. Stability and weight distribution in the lengthened tank was maintained by fitting longer tracks (each one composed of 83 track shoes instead of 79), and re-spacing the roadwheel bogies, which also resulted in lower ground pressure. Some modifications were made to the composite powerplant to simplify maintenance – the five separate water pumps were replaced by a single unit, for example – but it still had to be removed from the vehicle for many operations to be carried out (though the M4A4 was by no means alone in this). Some 7499 M4A4s were produced between July 1942 and September 1943, and only 56 of them stayed in the United States (though many were used there as training tanks before being extensively refurbished and sent on. The same was true for M4A2s); the vast majority went to the UK (and some were later transferred to other allies, such as China), where many were converted to become Sherman VC Fireflies, by the addition of the modified 17-pounder anti-tank gun (see below).

M4A6

One might be forgiven for thinking that four distinctly different powerplants was quite enough for one vehicle, but there were more yet to come. Late in 1942, the Caterpillar Tractor Co succeeded in modifying an adaptation of the Wright Cyclone air-cooled radial aero-engine known as the G200 to operate as a diesel, supercharged, but with direct fuel injection, rather than a carburettor. In fact, the D200 powerplant, as it became known, was very flexible indeed, and was really the forerunner of the more modern multi-fuel engine, for it would run on anything from crude oil to petrol, the latter mixed with engine oil in a 10:1 ratio. It developed its peak power, 450bhp, at the rather slow speed of 2000rpm, and was fitted with a transfer gearbox running at a ratio of 1.5:1 to avoid having to produce a new gearbox or final drive, which also allowed the drive shaft to be mounted low down in the hull, to improve the clearance between it and the floor of the turret. The lengthened hull of the M4A4 was chosen to house the new engine, and trials vehicles, designated as M4E1s, were thus built by Chrysler in Detroit.

The trials of the M4E1 went very well indeed, and on 23 January 1943 the Ordnance Committee ordered 775 of the engines, which it now designated the RD1820, fitted to M4A4 hulls, the new vehicle to be known as the M4A6 (the production-model powerplants were not interchangeable with the prototype versions, and the M4A6 was not identical with the M4E1). Production started at Detroit, using the cast upper hull front section from the later M4s together with the 'Mary Ann' profile cast final drive covers, and the first M4A6 left the Detroit Tank Arsenal on 28 October 1943. That winter, a policy decision to concentrate on the M4A3 was

M4A4 with the Chrysler A57 multibank engine

FACTS AND FIGURES

Crew	five
Weight	31.62 tonnes (31.1 tons)
Length	6.06m (19.8ft)
Width	2.9m (9.5ft)
Height	2.84m (9.33ft)
Max speed	40km/hr (25mph)
Max range	160km (100 miles)
Main armament	one 75mm M3 L/37
Powerplant	A57 30-cylinder multibank engine
Armour (front)	50mm (2in)
Armour (side)	38mm (1.5in)
Armour (rear)	38mm (1.5in)
Suspension type	vertical two-wheel bogies

GEARBOX AND TRANSMISSIONS

All the series-production M4 variants had the same manually operated synchromesh gearbox, with five forward and one reverse ratios. A variety of alternatives were proposed, and automatic units from Spicer and General Motors were tested, but not introduced. A combined transmission/brake/steering system, the EX100 Cross Drive, which permitted the tank to turn in its own length, as did the Merrit-Brown regenerative transmission/steering system fitted to some British tanks and the system copied from it and used in the German Tigers, was developed by General Motors; it was never introduced into the Sherman, but was to become the basis for similar systems installed in post-war American tanks starting with the M46 Patton.

There was considerable concern over the Sherman's agonisingly slow reverse gear, the low ratio being necessary to give respectable hill-climbing performance when going backwards. The solution tested was to fit an auxiliary planetary gear transfer box, which would have provided five forward and five reverse speeds. Trials were successful, but the war ended before the necessary modifications could be effected.

taken; the M4A6 production run was suspended in February 1944 after just 75 tanks had been produced.

M4A3E2 ASSAULT TANK

The only significantly up-armoured Sherman variant was the M4A3E2 Assault Tank, produced in small numbers – just 254 in all – in June and July 1944. An outline specification for a better-protected tank for use in the close support role had been put forward as early as May 1942 after an Anglo-American meeting held on 20 March had established a need for such a vehicle. The American contingent actually remained sceptical, but nonetheless, ALCO – which had not yet begun series production of M4s – was given the task of completing the design study and producing two pilots for what would become the Assault Tank, T14.

The hull was that of the standard welded M4, but increased in thickness in varying ways, and with the sponson side panels angled at 30 degrees. The powerplant was the Ford GAZ (a variant, as its designation indicates, of the GAA, and not to be confused with the Soviet truck manufacturer) and the standard transmission was used, save that the final drive ratio was increased from 2.84:1 to 3.57:1. Leaf spring suspension was suggested, but production difficulties resulted in the horizontal volute spring suspension together with the 654mm- (25.75in-) wide tracks from the still-born

M6 heavy tank being employed. Down to the level of the trunnion pins, the suspension was protected by 12.7mm (.5in) -thick armoured skirts. The lower hull sides, inside the track run, were 63mm (2.5in) thick, while the upper hull sides were 12.7mm (.5in) thinner, but were angled to compensate. The lower front was 100mm (4in) thick, thinning to half that in front of the drivers, where it was angled at 60 degrees; the rear armour was also 50mm (2in) thick. The turret, which was of a new design, was significantly bigger than that of the standard M4, though it turned on the same 1753mm (69in) ring. Its angled front face was 75mm (3in) thick, while its vertical side and rear walls were 25mm thicker. It carried the standard 75mm M3 gun in the M34A1 mount, though provision had been made for fitting the 76mm, 90mm or 105mm guns instead. The pilots were delivered in July and August; they weighed almost 47.7 tonnes (47 tons), thanks to the significant up-armouring and the heavier running gear, and had a top speed of 38kmh (24mph). Before the end of the year, the T14's brief career was over, Aberdeen having recommended that the project be cancelled, citing the extreme difficulty of maintenance and profound weaknesses in the running gear. The Armoured Force had never wanted the tank anyway, and outline agreements to produce them at the rate of 250 per month were hastily cancelled.

MODIFIED M4A3S

The need for an assault tank hadn't gone away, though – a fact which became increasingly clear as plans for the invasion of France were finalised. Time was of the essence, too, and eventually it was decided to satisfy the requirement by producing a small number of modified M4A3s, adding rolled armour plating to the hull and replacing the turret with a similarly dimensioned but more substantial version. An additional 37mm 1.5in) of plate was welded to the front upper glacis plate and the sponson sides, and a heavier final drive housing, 140mm (5.5in) thick, was cast. The new turret with 152mm- (6in-) thick verticals was cast, and fitted with an armoured cupola for the commander and the M62 mount used in the T20-series turret, with its gun shield increased to a thickness of 178mm (7in). It was originally intended to mount the 76mm gun, but eventually the 75mm gun was judged to be more flexible in the support role. The standard M4A3 powerplant and transmission were retained, but the final drive ratio was increased to 3.36:1, which reduced the top speed to 35kmh (22mph) but maintained reasonable acceleration even though the all-up weight was increased to 38.2 tonnes (37.5 tons). Ground pressure was kept to an acceptable 1.0kg/sq cm (14.2psi) by the use of extended 'duckbill' end connectors which increased the effective ground contact area by about 10 per cent. The 254 assault tanks produced were all made by Fisher, manufacture starting in May 1944 and deliveries concluding at the end of July. The first M4A3E2s began arriving in Europe in the autumn of

Above: The Ram tank, known officially as the M4A5, was manufactured in Canada using the much-modified hull of an M3 with a turret designed by L.E. Carr. It was armed with the two-pounder gun from the British Valentine. The lower hull comprised riveted armour plate, while the upper hull and turret were of cast armoured steel.

1944, in time for the winter battles before and during the ill-fated German offensive in the Ardennes, and the Rhine crossing, and were greeted with unanimous approval. An unspecified number of M4A3E2s were rearmed in the field with 76mm M1A2 guns – a relatively simple conversion, since the mounts were very similar. In early 1945, a plan to produce more M4A3E2s, with HVSS suspension and the 90mm gun, surfaced, but by that time the M26 Pershing was in production, and it was decided to concentrate on an assault version of that tank, with 152mm (6in) of frontal armour on the hull and 190mm (7.5in) on the turret, instead. It never reached volume production, and just 27 examples were built.

GRIZZLY

There was one M4 variant produced outside the United States. A heavily modified M3 – it was very different indeed in appearance, with a new upper hull and a turret for its main armament, both the work of L.E. Carr, who we last encountered designing the enlarged turret for the British

Medium M3s – was put into production in Montreal at the Canadian Pacific Railway Co's Angus Works, initially with the two-pounder gun from the British Valentine infantry tank (many of which were also built in Montreal; the majority of them were sent as aid to the Soviet Union) and later with the very much better six-pounder gun from later versions of that same tank. Known as the Ram I and Ram II, the tanks were in production from the end of 1941; none saw action (though variants, fitted out as command or observation posts, or, with their turrets removed, as personnel carriers and self-propelled guns did, in northwest Europe in 1944 and 1945; see below) but they proved invaluable to train crews who later went on to fight in Shermans. When the Ram production run came to an end in August 1943, after 55 Mark Is and 1899 Mark IIs had been produced, the Montreal production line switched over to assembling Sherman M4A1s, the only change being the substitution of British No. 19 radios for their American equivalent and fitting a two-inch bomb thrower/mortar in the turret – an addition which was later incorporated into American M4s. These tanks were known as Grizzly Mark Is, and a total of 188 were produced from parts mainly manufactured in the USA. Production ceased at the end of the year, by which time adequate supplies of Shermans were available directly from the US manufacturers. Like their predecessors, most Grizzlies were

Sherman Firefly

1 17-pounder gun
2 .30-calibre M1919 machine gun
3 .50-calibre M2 machine gun
4 Commander's cupola
5 Commander's periscope
6 Loader's hatch
7 Wireless set
8 Signal pistol
9 17pdr ammunition stowage
10 Commander's seat
11 Loader's seat
12 Escape hatch

13 Driver's periscope
14 Portable fire extinguisher
15 Driver's seat
16 Chrysler 425hp multibank petrol engine
17 Range finder
18 Two 12-volt batteries in series
19 Power train
20 Gearshift lever
21 Parking brake lever
22 Steering levers
23 Five-gallon water containers
24 Equipment chest
25 Ventilators
26 Radio antenna
27 First-aid box
28 3.5in thick gun shield
29 1.5in-thick mantlet
30 Binoculars
31 Periscope
32 Air cleaner manifold
33 Clutch assembly
34 Fan assembly
35 Radiator
36 Final drive housing
37 Track return rollers
38 Suspension bogie
39 Track drive sprocket
40 Track idler
41 Volute idler
42 2in bomb-thrower on loader's side of turret (not shown)

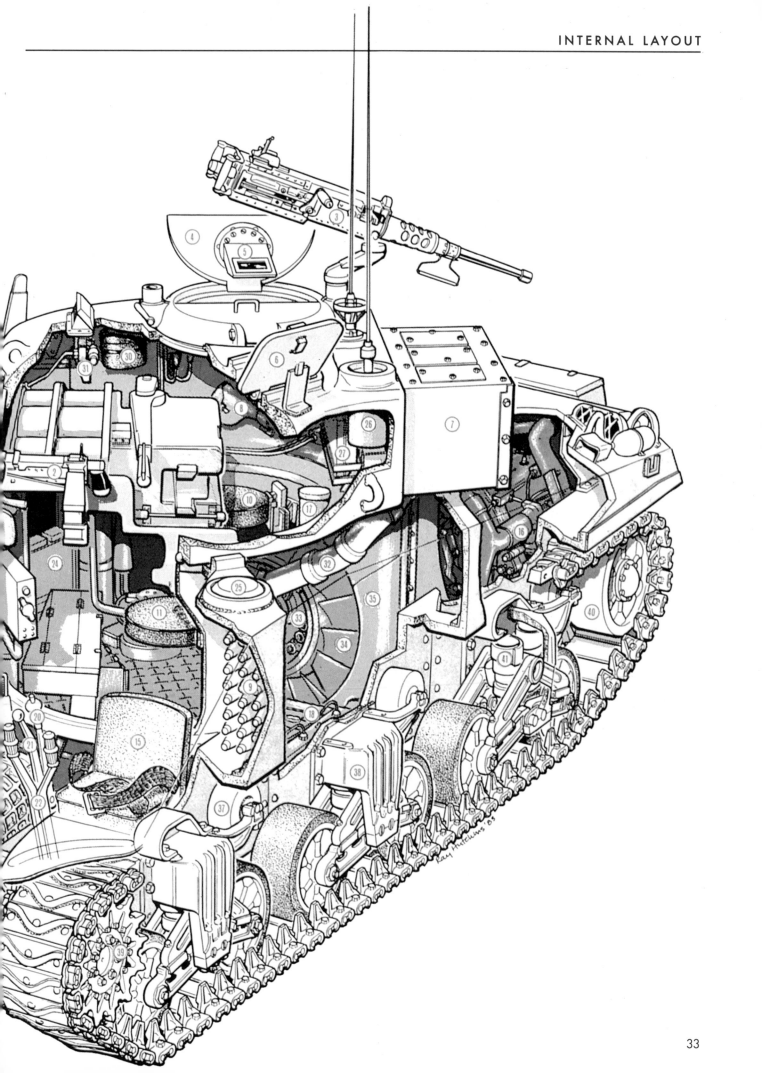

retained in Canada and used for training purposes, or converted for special purposes.

The most effective version of the M4, in terms of its ability to kill enemy tanks, was never used by American forces, and was devised and produced in the United Kingdom, combining existing Shermans (mostly Mark V/M4A4s) with the excellent 17-pounder towed anti-tank gun by what can only be described as brute force.

FIREFLY

The initial attempt to up-gun the tank succeeded (though only just) by the simple expedient of breaking all the rules – the gun was mounted rigidly in the mantlet, with no provision for recoil absorption, a solution which, many said, simply should not have worked. The engineer responsible, Major George Brighty, ordered three rounds fired from a safe distance with a rope lanyard; there seemed to be no damage done, so he climbed in and expended a further seven in the normal way. He emerged unscathed, but somewhat shaken by the experience, and convinced that such a vehicle could be developed, even if this particular version was not actually entirely practical.

When the War Office got to hear of his experiment, they forbade Brighty to continue with his work, but by that time it was painfully obvious that the Allies had to have a tank capable of dealing with the Tiger and the Panther, and that

Below: The M4A2 was distinguishable by the rear deck profile, modified to accept the General Motors diesel engine. Some 8053 were produced between April 1942 and May 1944, mostly for the UK and USSR.

meant one with the 17-pounder gun. An attempt to develop a stretched Cromwell with the 17-pounder in a bigger turret (the A30 Challenger) showed no signs of coming to useful fruition in time for the invasion, despite having been commenced back in 1942, and there was nothing for it but to return to the task of shoe-horning the gun into the Sherman.

It was decided to mount the gun, with its recoil mechanism intact this time, on raised trunnions in the original M34A1 mounting, which gave it an elevation range of +20 to -5 degrees. Despite being very short for its 76.2mm (3in) calibre, its breech was still almost 965mm (38in) long, and reached most of the way to the back of the turret; the recoil drove it into the bustle where the radio was installed, but that problem was solved by cutting out the rear of the bustle and adding an external armoured box to house the radio set, and this actually killed two birds with one stone, for it acted as a valuable counter-weight to the gun's long barrel at the same time. It remained to solve problems of flashback at the breech (by delaying the cycling of the semi-automatic action for a fraction of a second, until the residual pressure in the barrel had fallen to a safe level) and of ammunition handling (by turning the breech through 90 degrees around its axis, and cutting a second turret-top hatch to facilitate the loading of ammunition), and the new hybrid was ready for sustained testing.

On 30 December 1943 the decision was taken to modify precious Sherman Vs to what was to be called the Firefly configuration (and some Sherman Is were later converted, too), additionally deleting the hull machine gun and using the space it and its gunner occupied to hold 14 extra rounds

of ammunition, and thus was born the only American or British tank able to confront the Panthers and Tigers on anything like their own terms during the desperate fighting in 1944. The US Army was slow to become convinced of the need for a gun superior to the 75mm M3, even though it was demonstrated time after time, and steadfastly refused to have much to do with the Firefly concept, though Omar Bradley tried in vain to obtain some for his 12th Army Group in August 1944 and repeated his request the following February. They found their own M4s, even those fitted with the 76mm M1 cannon, severely undergunned, and thus unnecessarily vulnerable as a result. M4s which stayed in front-line US Army service until 1956 never had anything more powerful than the M1 gun, while those of some of the many other nations to employ it had the British 17-pounder, and Israel went further and fitted a French 105mm gun, amongst other modifications, to tanks which it used in battle as late as 1973.

Only in the lightly protected M36 tank-destroyer variant were the American Shermans to have a gun which would come close to matching those of the German Tigers and Panthers, and despite being considerably bigger in calibre, the 90mm gun with which it was armed was never the equal of the 17-pounder. During the European war, there were never enough Fireflies available to equip entire units; instead, they were mixed with 75mm gun-tanks, (and others with lesser guns, such as Cromwells) at the rate of one per troop (a unit of three tanks) originally, though that increased later, and were called up to deal with anything beyond their colleagues' capacity.

PLASTIC ARMOUR

Extra armour was also considered as a means of protecting the tank against hollow-charge man-portable weapons such as the Panzerfaust. The most promising was constructed of 255mm- (10in-) thick 'panels' of quartz gravel bound together with a mastic paste made from asphalt and wood flour, faced with 25mm (1in) of aluminium; panels were constructed to cover the sponsons and to fit around the sides and rear of the turret and hung from 12.7mm (.5in) steel wire attached to brackets welded on to the hull and turret. A complete kit weighed about eight tons, and could successfully defeat Panzerfaust or 8.5cm rockets as well as offering some protection against HEAT rounds, though conventional HE demonstrated an ability to sever the attachment cables, which sometimes resulted in the loss of an entire panel. The so-called 'plastic' armour also offered increased protection against armour-piercing rounds, but not as much as an equivalent weight of steel. Another method of defeating hollow-charge rockets was suggested – steel spikes, spaced around 63mm (2.5in) apart and around 203mm (8in) long, which penetrated the rocket's warhead and broke it up before it could detonate. The war was over before either of these innovations could be tested adequately.

Left: More M4A2s were built than any other M4 variant. In the year from May 1944, 2915 more were produced with 76mm gun, Type Two turret, wet ammunition storage, HVSS and centre-guided wide tracks.

CREW POSITIONS

As we have noted, the M4's crew were distributed two in the forward compartment and three in the turret. The driver and his assistant entered and left the tank through the hatches directly over their positions. Both were furnished with seats which could be raised, so that their heads emerged from the hatches, and this is how the tank was normally operated when not actually in combat. The driver was provided with a detachable hood-cum-windshield to be used in these circumstances. The first type had a double-glazed safety glass windshield, fitted with a wiper and defroster/demister, transparent plastic half-sides and light-gauge metal for the rest. Later it was decided that the screen should be foldable for stowage, and the sides, top and back were reworked in canvas. It was not as effective at keeping out rain, dust and wind as the earlier model, but had the advantage that the driver could climb in and out of the hatch with it in place. When not being use it was stored internally, above the transmission. Curiously, the same provision seems not to have been made for the assistant driver, as the other occupant of the forward compartment was officially known.

When closed-up, the driver and his assistant looked out of orientable M6 periscopes located in the hatch covers. Originally they were also provided with direct vision slots located in the front glacis plate just forward of the two access hatches, but these were deleted when it proved difficult to seal the gap around their covers against bullet splash; they were replaced by auxiliary M6 periscopes which were fixed in azimuth. M6 periscopes were simply paired prisms joined by a pressed-steel box, and frequently suffered from condensation. Just before the war's end they were replaced by the M13, which was a solid block of plastic with a reflecting surface at each end. Both types were identical in dimensions, their 'windows' being 47.5 x 152mm (1.88 x 6in) and their offset 255mm (10in).

The driver's controls consisted of pedals for clutch and accelerator (a hand throttle was also fitted) and paired steering levers, one for each track, which were floor-mounted close together and operated one in each hand. To the left, at eye-level when the seat was in the lower position, was an instrument and switch panel, while the gearshift lever and the (hand) parking brake (which was later replaced by a

pedal) were mounted on the side of the transmission cover, to his right. It took considerable dexterity to handle the controls of the Cletrac (so named because it was developed by the Cleveland Tractor Co) controlled differential steering smoothly, but apart from that, driving the tank was like driving any heavy wheeled vehicle. The minimum turning circle was of the order of 20m (65ft), which meant that the Sherman was under a considerable disadvantage on mountain roads and even in the older towns and villages it would encounter in Europe, with their narrow streets and sharp turns. Compared with the (considerably longer) British Churchill or German Tiger, both of which could spin around while stationary, and thus turn literally in their own length, they were very unwieldy indeed, and often had to take two or three bites at a hairpin bend.

The various automatic gearboxes which were tried out in trials certainly made the driver's job easier, but not one was fitted to operational tanks. Better still (at least, eventually) was the General Motors EX100 Cross Drive combined automatic transmission, steering and braking system which

Below: The 75mm gun-armed M4A3 entered production in June 1942, and 1690 had been produced by September 1943. This late-production tank had no vision slots but had its gun in the modified M34A1 mount.

Above: From February 1944, 75mm-armed M4A3 tanks were produced with wet ammunition storage, and a total of 3071 were to be built over 1945. The M4A3 variant was the definitive Sherman in US service.

was developed while the Sherman was in production but likewise was only ever fitted to one tank, an M4A3, for the purposes of testing. There were considerable delays in the development programme, and it was actually 1947, by which time the Sherman had long gone out of production, before the new system, now designated the CD-850-1, was ready to go into a production tank; it was fitted to the M46 Patton, a development of the wartime M26 Pershing, where it was very successful indeed.

The Cross Drive actually belonged to another, later, era, but a simple explanation of the principle on which it worked will serve to highlight just what an improvement over the old controlled differential it was. The drive was split into two components, one transmitted hydraulically, via the torque convertor, the other mechanically. The hydraulic component always went to both tracks equally, but the mechanically transmitted component could be switched between the tracks by means of a controlled differential (which was now hydraulically actuated), thus providing more power to the 'outside' track and turning the tank away from it. The differential was controlled by a short joystick, and thus steering the tank was the work of but one hand, and required very little physical effort. Moving it to one side or the other when the transmission was in neutral caused the tracks to move in opposite directions, spinning the tank around in its own length. The advantages over the mechanical system the Sherman (and most of its contemporaries) used were so great that it is curious that greater effort was not put into perfecting it sooner; after all, both Germany and the UK had

similar systems in service by the time the Sherman was conceived.

THE BOW GUNNER'S POSITION

The assistant driver/bow gunner's position was a mirror-image of the drivers, but without the controls and instrument panel. Instead, off-set somewhat to the right, he had the pistol grip and breech of the .30in-calibre M1919A4 air-cooled, belt-fed machine gun which was located in the glacis plate in a ball mount, and could be traversed through 20 degrees to the left and 25 degrees to the right, could be elevated through 20 degrees and depressed through 10 degrees. The gunner aimed by means of a sight vane forward of the periscope, which was linked mechanically to the gun, or by a combination of instinct and tracer rounds. In command and headquarters tanks, the bow gunner also operated the SCR 506 radio, used for voice- and morse code communication between higher echelons, which was housed in the sponson just behind his right shoulder – in the place a main gun ammunition storage box occupied in a fighting vehicle.

The gunner's position was in the right front of the turret, alongside the gun, facing forwards. Initially he had no direct-vision sight, but had to rely on the periscope gunsight mounted in the turret roof. There soon proved to be insurmountable problems in maintaining the alignment between

Left: M4A3s – a total of 4542 of them – were produced between March 1944 and April 1945 with the Type Two turret and 76mm gun. This model was the first to be fitted with HVSS and centre-guided, wider track. Note the front plate set at 47 degrees.

Right: The fourth version of the M4A3 was the up-armoured -E2 assault tank, which weighed eight tons more thanks to its thickened frontal armour and new heavier turret. Just 254 were built. Note the track grousers or extensions fitted to reduce ground pressure.

the periscope sight and the gun tube, and the gun mounting was modified and the mounting plate pierced to the right of the gun tube to accept a direct sight, the rotor cover being extended to protect it. Then, in a 75mm tank he was provided with an M55 telescope (or an essentially similar M51 for tanks fitted with 76mm guns or 105mm howitzers), which gave 3x magnification and a field of view of just over 12 degrees (the 76mm gun-tanks later got a more powerful telescope, the M71, with 5x magnification, which was better matched to their longer range). The M4 periscope provided for the gunners of early production M4A1 tanks was equipped with a 1.44x magnification M38 telescope, with a ballistic reticle. Later 75mm tanks were fitted with M4A1 periscopes with M38A2 telescopes, of similar power but with much better optical qualities. The later periscopes could also be equipped with telescopes better suited to the two other main weapons, either the M47A2 or the M77C, the former with slightly greater magnification, the latter with a greater field of view. Almost at the end of World War II, these periscopes were superseded by the M10, which had paired telescopes, one with simple optics and a field of 42 degrees horizontally and eight degrees vertically, for use against targets close at hand, the other with 6x magnification and an 11-degree field of view, for use against distant targets.

THE GUNNER

He laid the gun onto the target indicated by the commander by traversing the turret and elevating (or depressing) the gun in the mount. There were three types of power traverse fitted to M4-series tanks, not necessarily according to type, but rather according to availability, and one, produced by the Oilgear Co, was markedly superior to the others – a similar hydraulic unit from Logansport and an electrically powered

system from Westinghouse. All were completely independent of the main powerplant, the hydraulic systems being powered by electric motors which also supplied power to the gyrostabiliser system pump. The controls for all three types were basic similar, and were hand-operated. A back-up manual system was installed, operated by a handwheel (this was the only means of traversing the original 105mm howitzer-equipped turrets), and a similar wheel was used to elevate or depress the gun via a simple worm drive and reduction gearing. One of the Sherman's main strengths was the speed at which the turret could be traversed – a full revolution took only 10 seconds. Compared with the minimum of 25 seconds it took a Tiger to traverse through 360 degrees (and at worst, that operation took a whole minute), this was very fast indeed, and often allowed a Sherman to get off one, two or even more shots at an adversary while he was still struggling to bring his gun to bear – frequently a decisive advantage.

FIRING THE M4'S GUNS

All the main guns fitted to M4-series tanks were set off mechanically, by means of the impact of a spring-loaded firing pin on a percussion cap, though the action was initiated electrically. The gunner fired both the main gun and the co-axial machine gun via switches conveniently placed for either the elevating handwheel or the control for the power traverse (the actual arrangement varied somewhat, according to which traverse system was installed), and a foot pedal trigger was installed, too. As well as the sight, he was furnished with an azimuth indicator, a gunner's quadrant, which told the gun tube's elevation, and a compass. Using these three instruments he could fire indirectly onto a target outside his vision range, at least in theory. In practice, a

magnetic compass which would work reliably inside the tank was never developed, and the best one could hope for was a reading accurate to +20 or -20 degrees, which made indirect fire on a compass bearing questionable, to say the least.

THE LOADER

The loader's primary function was to keep both the main gun and the co-axial machine gun in working order and supplied with ammunition. He was located to the left of the gun's breech, opposite the gunner, and, in common with most of his sort, had more room than any other member of the tank's crew, largely because he was obliged to reach the rounds stored in locations all around the central portion of the tank. The ready ammunition in the early welded-hull production tanks consisted of eight rounds laid flat on the floor of the turret basket and a further 12 racked vertically against the rear, below the SCR 508 radio installed in the turret bustle. A further 47 rounds were located in the three sponson storage boxes, and 30 more were in a box below the turret basket floor, to the rear of the belly escape hatch, for a total of 97 rounds. The .30in ammunition was stored belted, in boxes, literally all around the tank, in the sponsons and in the floor, as was .50in ammunition if an M2 machine gun were fitted at the commander's hatch. The .45in ammunition for the single sub-machine gun was carried in magazines, clipped to the rear of the turret roof, above the radio set, and there was room for a box of hand grenades underneath the gunner's seat. The load of ammunition for the main gun varied; cast-hulled M4s carried seven fewer rounds than tanks with welded hulls, M4A3s with 75mm guns adapted for wet stowage carried seven more. Tanks with 76mm guns (which were all fitted with wet stowage compartments) carried 71 rounds, and those with 105mm howitzers, 66 rounds. Fireflies carried 77 or 78 rounds of 17-pounder ammunition, arranged very differently – five rounds in ready baskets on the turret floor, 14 where the bow gunner sat in other tanks and 58 or 59 in three bins below the turret basket. The mix of different ammunition types – AP, HE and smoke for the 75mm and 76mm guns; HE, HEAT (high-explosive, anti-tank) shaped-charge rounds and smoke for the 105mm guns – varied according to conditions, the type of combat and the efficiency of the logistical system which delivered them to combat units.

The breeches of the guns fitted to Shermans were turned on their sides, so that the breech blocks moved horizontally, which made the loader's task somewhat easier, but even so, his job was hard work – a single round of 75mm APCBC ammunition weighed almost 9kg (20lb), one of 76mm, almost 11.5kg (25lb), and one for a 17-pounder gun, more than 17kg (38lb). A high-explosive 105mm round was even heavier still, at more than 19kg (42lb). The loader also had responsibility for the operation of the bomb thrower, which

Above: The fifth version of the M4A3 was an infantry support tank, fitted with the 105mm howitzer. A total of 3039 were built between May 1944 and Jun 1945, and this tank was one of the first batch.

was mounted in the left front of the turret roof at a fixed angle of 35 degrees. The launcher could be set for 32, 68 or 137 metres (35, 75 or 150 yards), the shorter ranges being obtained by bleeding off some of the propellant gases. It was intended primarily to establish smoke screens, but could be used to launch any standard two-inch mortar round. He was provided with an M6 periscope in an orientable mounting, and in some tanks had a pistol/grenade port in the left turret wall (there was a great deal of controversy about this item; some authorities rated it as vital, others believed it only served to weaken the integrity of the turret armour. They were probably both right in equal measure, but there was certainly no denying its attractiveness in close-quarters battle, when sappers might otherwise be able to approach the tank and place a satchel charge with relative impunity. It was deleted and reinstated more than once, as a result. Alternative defences against close-quarters infantry attack were suggested and tested; see below).

The tank's commander sat behind the gunner and slightly above him when the tank was closed up, on a seat which could be raised, like those of the driver and his assistant, so

that he could expose his head and upper torso in the hatch. He had a pair of vanes, one on the front turret roof, next to the gunner's periscope, the other on the turret hatch flap in front of his own periscope, through which he could align them with a target (the arrangement was modified in later tanks, the two vanes being located together towards the front of the turret; the commander could then make use of them either via the periscope or directly). The commander also had direct control over the turret's traverse, and thus could lay the gun in the general direction of a target himself, leaving the gunner to aim precisely.

THE COMMANDER

He himself had charge of the short-range FM (frequency modulated) SCR 508 radio in the turret bustle, which he used to communicate both with his echelon commander and with other tanks in his unit (the radio also incorporated the interphone system, by means of which the five members of the crew communicated, the high noise levels inside making normal speech impossible). This voice-only set operated in line of sight, and had a theoretical range of up to 32km (20 miles), though that was seldom achieved in practice, and 10-13km (six to eight miles) was a more reasonable estimate. Company commanders also had AM (amplitude modulated) SCR 506 sets installed in their tanks. They occupied the

position of the 17-round main gun ammunition storage box in the front of the right-hand sponson, and were operated by the assistant driver/bow gunner. These sets could send and receive voice or morse code, the former over up to 80km (50 miles), the latter over perhaps twice that distance.

Where an anti-aircraft machine gun was fitted, the commander would operate it himself. There was a certain degree of controversy over how effective this weapon really was, considering that the commander could only fire it when he was exposed in the hatch; it was often omitted from British Shermans. Certainly, the .50in M2 machine gun was much more effective than the .30in M1919 specified originally. The mounting allowed two different elevation ranges, depending on whether it held the gun in its forward or rear position: +56 degrees to -25 degrees in the former; +80 degrees to -36 degrees in the latter, which allowed an intrepid commander to engage a dive bomber.

In the new turret developed for the T20-series tanks, which were fitted to the later Shermans, the commander was provided with an armoured cupola with 152mm- (6in-) vision blocks which permitted him to see out directly without exposing himself. This turret had a loader's hatch, and the third machine gun was often mounted there. The armoured vision cupola was subsequently also fitted to new production and re-manufactured 75mm-gun-tanks with the original turret.

Above: Almost the entire production of the M4A4 Sherman, 7499 of which were built between July 1942 and September 1943, went to the British Army, which re-christened it the Sherman V.

SUSPENSION MODIFICATIONS

As we have seen, the original suspension system, taken directly from the much lighter Medium Tank, M2, soon proved to be deficient, and was strengthened by increasing the size of its vertical volute springs (a volute spring is perhaps best described as a coiled leaf spring, attached at its extremities, like the main spring of a clock; in this application the spring coil was drawn out sideways, as it were, to form a truncated cone, which was mounted base upwards), but this was still only marginally within the acceptable limits. Clearly, the performance of the suspension would have to be improved, but not at the cost of re-engineering the tank as a whole – the replacement system would have to be very similar in character. In the original, the lower end of the springs rested on the tops of the two rigidly mounted arms which carried the 230mm- (9in-) wide wheels, and was held in compression against the mounting point on the hull. The replacement, delivered for testing in April 1943, simply turned the springs through 90 degrees, so that they now lay horizontally, and acted between extensions to the two arms, which now worked against each other, scissors fashion. Shock absorbers were incorporated, mounted above the springs to damp the action. Now, when one of the roadwheels was deflected upwards, part of the load was transmitted to the other by the springs, which automatically kept up the tension on the track. The modification improved the rough-ground performance appreciably, but did nothing to reduce excessive wear on the rubber-tyred roadwheels and left the ground pressure – which was also giving cause for concern – unchanged; it was deemed to be insufficient an improvement to warrant the cost of re-tooling, and the designers went back to their drawing boards.

Six months later, a revised arrangement which used dual 160mm- (6.25in-) wide roadwheels on each arm of the bogie, the guide teeth on the track running between them rather than at the outer extremities, which allowed the track to be widened considerably (from 421mm to 585mm [16.56in to 23in]), was presented for evaluation, together with suitably redesigned track, return rollers, drive sprockets and idlers. Even though the new suspension and track increased the total weight of the tank (by almost 1.52 tonnes [1.5 tons] when single-pin T66 track shoes were used; by almost 2.54 tonnes [2.5 tons] with much more robust dual-pin T80 track shoes) ground pressure was reduced by around 30 per cent (that of the M4A2(76)W, which weighed 33.36 tonnes [32.8 tons], was 1.06kg/sq cm [15.1psi]; that of the M4A3(76)W HVSS, which weighed 33.73 tonnes [33.1 tons] with T66 track, was 0.77kg/sq cm [11psi]), while rough ground stability was even better than that which the early HVSS version had demonstrated. The new system was adopted at the end of March 1944.

WIDER TRACKS

At least three types of 'grousers' – track shoe extensions which broaden the track way beyond their original dimensions, and which are sometimes necessary in very soft going – were developed for the Sherman, the most spectacular of them increasing the width of the T80 track to 990mm (39in) and reducing the ground pressure exerted by a late-model M4A3 to just 0.49kg/sq cm (7psi), even though the extensions themselves added over two tonnes (1.97 tons) to the tank's all-up weight. In February 1944 Chrysler was tasked with producing a modification to the mountings of the running gear to allow the original 421mm- (16in-) wide narrow track to space it out from the hull by 115mm (4.5in) on each side, to allow 'duck-bill' end connectors to be fitted to both the inside and the outside of the track links; each extended the track width by 90mm (3.56in), which increased the effective width of the narrow tracks to 585mm (23.69in) and reduced ground pressure to around 0.7kg/sq cm (10psi). The system was adopted for re-manufactured tanks and kits were made up to permit modifications to existing vehicles to be performed in field workshops from August 1944.

Below: Many British Sherman Vs were modified to the Firefly configuration, the original 75mm gun being replaced by the long-barrelled high-velocity 17-pounder. This model was equal (in firepower at least) to the German Panthers and Tigers it met after D-Day.

Right: Just 75 M4A4 hulls were fitted with RD-1820 radial diesel engines and designated M4A6s. Note the later-type one-piece cast hull front section and the additional armour over the ammunition stowage.

Suspension bogies with twin horizontal volute springs, developed by Allis Chalmers for the T22 heavy tractor, together with 559mm- (22in-) wide tracks were fitted to an M4A4 for trials purposes. It was soon concluded that they were inadequate to support the tank's weight. Bogies with paired double coiled springs in place of the horizontal volute springs, developed by Horstmann in England for a railway application, were fitted to a Sherman V in Canada, and proved to be satisfactory in terms of performance but inadequately reliable. That experiment, too, was abandoned. Long bogies as fitted to a heavy half-track tractor produced by the Diamond T Co were mooted and rejected, as were bogies incorporating leaf springs.

Another, much more radical, design study, which eventually came to nothing as far as the M4 was concerned but which had consequences for the wider tank development programme, saw a pair of M4A2s fitted with torsion bar suspension and six dual 660mm (26in) roadwheels per side; when loaded to 36 tonnes (35.3 tons), the ground pressure they exerted was only marginally over 0.7kg/sq cm (10psi) on 610mm (24in) tracks, and rough ground performance was well within acceptable limits (the system permitted up to 178mm [7in] of vertical movement, but that was restricted to 125mm [5in] by volute-spring bump stops). The torsion bar

system was never considered for application to the M4, but it was to be adopted for future American medium/heavy tanks, starting with the M26 Pershing, and was to continue through the Patton series, culminating in the M60 Main Battle Tank, and on into the M1A1 Abrams, the current US Army main battle tank.

In one particular area the Sherman was very vulnerable. As we have observed, main gun ammunition was stored in boxes in the sponsons, two to the right of the hull and one to the left, and combat experience showed that a significant number of losses resulted from ammunition fires started by penetration of the armour in these areas. As an interim solution, simple plates, 25mm (1in) thick, were welded onto the outer surface over the vulnerable areas to provide extra protection; the modification was first made in the field, but was later applied during manufacture. It was deleted after wet storage for main gun ammunition was introduced in 1944.

Appliqué armour was also employed to improve the protection of the front of the hull and turret. In particular, in the right/front corner of the interior of the latter, part of the metal was machined away to improve access to the gun controls. Eventually, the turret itself was redesigned to take account of this, but as an interim measure, shaped external

patches 37mm (1.5in) thick were welded on to protect the affected area. Similarly, patches were also applied to the front surface of the fairings for the drivers' hatches. Like the patches over the ammunition storage areas, these modifications were first carried out in the field, and later on the production lines. Many tank crews carried large quantities of 'spare' track shoes tack-welded to their vehicles to act as expedient armour, though that practice wasn't limited to Shermans, of course.

PROTECTION FROM CLOSE-QUARTERS ATTACK

We have noted how there was some controversy surrounding the effectiveness of the pistol port situated in the original M4 turret, adjacent to the loader's position, and it is certainly true that it represented a potential weakness in the integrity of the armour, but when it was deleted the crew of the tank were defenceless against attack by infantrymen and pioneers who managed to approach to within metres of the tank and thus actually gain its protection. Isolated tanks were, of course, particularly vulnerable in this way. When tanks first went to war, in 1916, they were in real danger from close-quarters attack by determined infantrymen, and not a few were disabled by rudimentary satchel charges (often no more sophisticated than half a dozen hand

Above: The M4A6's hull was that of the M4A4, and the chief difference between the two vehicles was the bulge in the rear deck. The M4A6 was discontinued due to standardisation; none saw service.

grenades in a gunny sack) exploded under their tracks. The same tactics were used successfully during World War II, too, and were supplemented by magnetic mines and so-called 'lunge' mines or pole mines. The latter, which consisted of a hollow charge fixed to the end of a short pole, which was rammed against the tank's hull with a movement akin to a bayonet thrust, was invariably fatal to the attacker, and was employed exclusively by the Japanese. Attacks on Sherman tanks with magnetic mines were never common enough to warrant the emulation of German practice, which consisted of coating the tank's hull and turret with a non-conductive layer (the German version, known as *zimmerit* paste, was a woodchip-filled mastic), though tank crews sometimes gave their vehicles a partial coat of cement, usually applied with a trowel to hull front and sides. Those responsible for the Sherman improvement programme regularly reviewed methods of combating these tactics, ranging from ways of employing anti-personnel mines and grenades and flame-weapons to methods of firing sub-machine guns from within the tank without resorting to cutting holes in its sides.

The means of achieving the latter was somewhat bizarre, though the Americans were not alone in considering it – there was a rather better-known attempt made in Germany, too, though whether with the same end exclusively in mind is unclear. It consisted of a heavy steel tube, bent around a shallow curve to 90 degrees, which fitted over the muzzle of an M3 sub-machine gun. Together with a dedicated periscope equipped with a simple sight, this tube could be fitted in place of a standard traversing periscope (and thus could be employed by the commander, the loader or even the assistant driver/bow gunner) in a rudimentary elevating mount. In use, it couldn't have been simpler: one inserted the muzzle of the sub-machine gun into the lower end of the tube, sighted through the periscope and pressed the trigger. The tube – which was cut out on its inner radius as far as its end, to prevent fouling – deflected the fire. Tests demonstrated that it was effective against silhouette targets out to around 30m (100ft), though there is no evidence that it was ever used in combat. The German version of the same device – the *Maschinenpistole mit Vorsatz*, or *Maschinenpistole mit Krummlauf* as it was known ('Vorsatz' means 'design'; the letter J, P or V was added, distinguishing between the three sub-variants. 'Krummlauf' means 'in a curved path') was altogether more serious. One variant, the MP44K/30, had a 30-degree bend in the barrel, another, the MP44K/40 (which seems to have been no more than a paper exercise), a 40-degree bend and the third, the MP44K/90, turned the projectile through a full right-angle. It wasn't enough simply to bend the barrel and fit mirror sights, of course; gas vents were also drilled into it to allow propellant gas to be expelled progressively, reducing the muzzle velocity from 650m per second (2130ft per second) to little over 300m per second (985ft per second) in the process, which certainly ensured that the weapon would never have been of any use at anything but quite short ranges. It is said that as many as 10,000 MP44K/30s were ordered (and certainly, there are many examples in museums and perhaps even in private collections), but there is little evidence of it seeing action.

Rather less unconventional were the experiments aimed at mounting command-detonated explosive devices at strategic points on the tank's hull. The first of these employed the Mark IIA1 hand grenade (its designation was at variance with normal US practice), the infantryman's standard defensive fragmentation grenade, adopted in 1917. It consisted of a cast-iron body, deeply incised so that it would break up the more easily, filled with 21g (.75oz) of the sort of explosive used as the propellant in small-arms ammunition. It had a four and a half second delay fuse, and was (rather unpredictably) lethal out to a radius of perhaps 15m (50ft). Later, the grenades were replaced with M2A3 or M3 anti-personnel mines. The former were an early (and not too efficient) version of the claymore mine, which used plastic explosive as the propellant and iron pellets as the destructive element;

Below: An M4, its R975 radial engine being replaced. Many early Shermans were lost due to ammunition fires, so armour plating was welded to vulnerable areas, two of the patches being visible here.

the latter were more ambitious, based on a modified version of the M49A2 60mm mortar shell, which contained almost 1.4kg (three pounds) of high-explosive. All three types were fixed at various points around the lower hull of the tank, and fired from a control panel mounted between the two drivers, above the transmission housing. Another experimental device consisted of sections of piping, filled with high explosive and mounted on the sponsons and around the turret. All the devices were considered to be highly dangerous to supporting infantry, and as soon as it became obvious that the protection they afforded was inferior to that supplied by such forces, the experiments were discontinued.

Flame-weapons were held to offer a greater degree of controllability and flexibility, and the best of them developed for close-quarters defensive purposes against infantry and enemy positions, rather than as offensive weapons, was probably the Anti-personnel Flame Projector, E1. Basically, this was a tank containing 3.8l (0.8 Imp gal/one US gal) of phosphorous/phosphorous sesquisulfide mixture which combusts spontaneously. Projectors were mounted at the tank's four corners, just above the track run, and each one produced a fan-shaped burst of flame out to about 15m (50ft). The 'fuel' supply was enough for 20-30 bursts, and the projectors could be employed together or separately at will. Known as Scorpion (and later Skink, so as not to be confused

with the chain-flail mine exploder of the same name, though then it came into conflict with the similarly named Canadian Grizzly-based light AA tank, see below), the devices were tested in early 1945, but were never fitted to operational tanks during World War II.

WET AMMUNITION STORAGE

We have observed that the practice of storing main gun ammunition in the sponsons, where it was protected by only 37mm (one and a half inches) of armour, led to the loss of far too many tanks, and that armour patches were applied over the vital areas, but this was only a stop-gap solution. The definitive answer was to be to store the ammunition in water-filled tanks in the bowels of the vehicle, and this required a major redesign which began in July, 1943. In all, plans for modifications to seven types of Sherman gun-tank were drawn up – for the M4A3 with all three types of gun (the 75mm M3, the 76mm M1A1 and the 105mm M4), for the M4 with the 76mm and 105mm guns, and for the 76mm-armed M4A1 and -A2. In the 75mm- and 76mm-armed tanks, the ammunition storage was moved to tanks below the turret floor. Ten boxes, each of which held 10 rounds of 75mm ammunition, could be located there, each of them filled with 14l (3.1 Imp gal/3.7 US gal) of water with ethylene glycol added as an anti-freeze and with corrosion inhibitors to prevent rust forming. A further four rounds on the turret floor in a ready rack were also water-protected. The larger physical size of the 76mm rounds meant that a tank with the more powerful gun could carry a total of 65 rounds in the lower hull and a further six in the ready-ammunition box. Wet storage boxes were not supplied for the 105mm-armed tanks (all the 105mm rounds except the HEAT were semi-fixed, so that their propellant charge could be varied, and they were thus not watertight), but armoured racks were provided instead, with a capacity of 66 rounds.

In order for the loader to be able to reach the under-floor storage, much of the turret basket was cut away, which had the additional benefit of improve access to the driving compartment from the fighting compartment (eventually it was to be deleted entirely, and the seats for the turret crew were then suspended on brackets from the turret ring, rather than being pedestal-mounted). Other improvements included the re-profiled and thickened glacis plate, the 'Mary Ann' nose casting, a comprehensive redesign of the driver's position and the addition of the armoured cupola for the commander.

Right: Operational Shermans were fitted with three different types of suspension and track. The earliest tanks had return rollers mounted vertically in the bogies, but when heavier springs were fitted, it was found necessary to move them back and add a skid plate. The final solution was to replace the vetical volute springs with horizontally mounted units, and at the same time, the track width was increased from 420mm (16.5in) to 585mm (23in), which improved soft-ground performance significantly.

Chrysler built pilots of each of the seven versions of the tank; the work on the hulls was completed by early February 1944, but by that time the Pressed Steel Car Co had already built 100 M4A1(76)Ws. These early models mounted the M1A1 gun, which had no muzzle brake, but that was soon replaced by the M1A1C or the M1A2, which had. In all, a total of 3426 of these vehicles were to be delivered by the end of the war; later models were fitted with the HVSS suspension and wide, centre-guided track. The dry-stowage M4A2 stayed in production until May, and was then superseded by the M4A2(76)W, most of the total of 2915 of which were produced at Fisher (most went to the Soviet Union). Fisher also produced the wet-stowage M4A3, with the 75mm gun and many of the 4542 M4A3(76)Ws, the balance being supplied from the Chrysler-run Detroit Tank Arsenal, where the revised 105mm version was also produced.

THE M7 GUN

The original equipment specification for the M4s had envisaged a more powerful gun than the 75mm M3 being fitted to the tank, and as we have seen, the turret face plate was made demountable as a result. The 76.2mm M7 gun had considerably better armour-piercing potential than the M3, but was considered to be too heavy, at 905kg (1990lb), to be installed in the medium tank's turret. Instead, a programme to develop a new gun in the same calibre (together with a new round for it) was initiated. The result was the 518kg (1140lb) T1, which was designed with the same breech ring assembly as the M3, so that it would fit in the same M34 mount. Two examples were manufactured, and one was installed in the turret of an M4A1 in August, 1942. It was badly out of balance, and this was corrected by sawing 380mm (15in) off the muzzle of the 57-calibre- (ie, 4343mm/171in) long barrel and adding weight at the breech. Firing tests were completed successfully, and the new gun was declared satisfactory and standardised as the 76mm Gun, M1. The M1 was then fitted to an M4A1 (with a spacer plate in the turret face plate to move it forward 50mm (2in), to prevent the recoil guard interfering with the bustle-mounted radio), and plans were drawn up to manufac-

ture 1000 of what was to have become the M4A1(76M1); extended trials soon revealed that there was a problem in traversing the turret, particularly when the tank was on a slope, though this could be cured by adding a 365kg (800lb) counter-weight in the form of an external armoured storage locker to the rear of the turret. Twelve M4A1(76M1)s were produced at the Pressed Steel Car Co plant, and a final report on their performance was submitted to the Ordnance Committee on 5 April 1943. The Armoured Force rejected the tank due to the inadequate space in the turret, calling it a 'quick fix' improvised from existing components. The contract to produce 17 more (enough, all told, to equip a tank company) was cancelled; three of the existing tanks were retained and the remaining nine were ordered reconverted back to the original M4A1 specification. Less than perfect though the 76mm gun in the smaller turret was, the conversion was approved later, after the Normandy landings, when it became clear that the extra firepower was essential, though it seems that few modifications were actually carried out.

THE M4E6 MODEL

The same 3 May meeting (at which wet stowage of ammunition was also recommended) of the Ordnance Committee which consigned the M4A1(76M1) to the dustbin also recommended that two pilots of an improved model be produced. These were to carry the M1 gun in a modified mount, the T80, in the bigger turret designed for the T20-series tanks then in the prototype stage, which was based on the same 1753mm- (69in-) diameter turret ring. The tank thus modified was known as the M4E6, and testing commenced in July. By mid-August it was clear that this approach worked, and it was recommended that the M4E6 model be adopted for future production of 76mm-gun-tanks. Later, improved ammunition, including the HVAP (hyper-velocity armour-piercing) round, was developed, and the performance of the M1 gun was also improved by modifying the rifling to impart greater spin to the projectile, but it was still never to match the British 17-pounder Mark IV and Mark VII guns, as fitted to the Sherman Fireflies. Discarding-sabot ammunition devel-

oped for the 17-pounder guns in the last year of the war made them even more powerful; with the SVDS round, one could pierce 190mm (7.5in) of homogeneous armour at a 30-degree angle at a range of 900m (1000yds) – something the best 76mm round, the M93 HVAP, was hard pressed to achieve at one-fifth of that distance.

SHERMAN GUN-TANKS

Shortly after initial Sherman production got underway in early 1942, work began on the development of a suitable mount for the 105mm howitzer. Prototypes were installed in a pair of M4A4s, and testing began at Aberdeen and Fort Knox just before the year's end. It was soon obvious that though the variant was desirable, the installation was unacceptable, and a comprehensive redesign of the gun itself was ordered; power traverse and gyrostabilisation were deleted in the interests of simplicity, and were only restored much later. It was August 1943 before the revamped tank was ready for testing, but the lengthy delay was vindicated, because the new, lightened, shortened gun in its modified mount was accepted immediately, and standardised as the 105mm Howitzer, M4. The first M4(105) tanks were delivered in February 1944, and M4A3(105)s followed in May. A total of 4680 were produced in all.

By the time of the Normandy landings, in June 1944, the Sherman gun-tanks were available in huge numbers, and were to play a pre-eminent role in the savage fighting which followed the securing of the beachhead, as the American, British and Canadian armies battled their way across northern France, through Belgium and into Germany. They weren't the only effective tanks the Allies had, far from it, but more importantly they were by far the most numerous, and by then they had also spawned a wide range of support variants, from tank destroyers and gun carriages to engineering vehicles, various mine exploders, armoured recovery tractors, personnel carriers and command and observation posts, as well as specialist vehicles devised specifically to fight their way ashore in opposed amphibious operations, as we shall see.

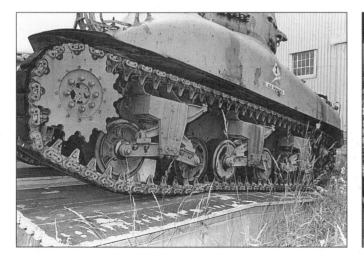

CHAPTER 3

The Sherman in Action

The Sherman tank was built on the 'jeep' principle which played such an important part in US strategy – this meant they were relatively cheap and quick to produce, and could be turned out in large numbers. It was this numerical superiority, not any virtue of design, which made the M4 tank such a devasting weapon.

When Tobruk fell to Rommel's forces on 21 June 1942, it seemed distinctly possible that the British in Egypt would be unable to hold the Axis troops short of the Suez Canal; that raised the spectre of Axis armies from north and south linking up east of the Mediterranean, threatening the oilfields of Iraq and much more. British Prime Minister Winston Churchill was in Washington, at the time, and in answer to US President Franklin Roosevelt's offer of help, asked specifically for M4 Sherman tanks, the first examples of which had come off the production lines some four months before. Whilst the first two M4A1s had been shipped to the UK, the bulk of the new production already delivered had gone to the US Army, and now these tanks would have to be employed to stop Rommel.

HASTY PLANNING

The first, hastily thrown together plan called for the US 2nd Armoured Division under Gen George Patton, then training at the Desert Warfare Center in California, to be shipped to Egypt to go into combat alongside the British and Empire forces, but it soon became clear that it would be October or even November before they could be expected to arrive, which may well have been too late. Instead, they gave up their tanks and these were quickly sent east by train.

A convoy of ships was assembled, and left the USA on 15 July. One ship was sunk by a submarine the following day,

Left: So heavily camouflaged with foliage that it is impossible to determine its type, an M4 of the British 4th Armoured Division moves through Normandy. The banks lining the road were to prove a major obstacle.

and a replacement was dispatched with 52 more tanks aboard to make up the numbers. By 11 September, a total of 318 (actually 319 if we count the second prototype M4A1, sent from the UK to Alexandria in August to allow troops, particularly workshop personnel, to begin to familiarise themselves with the new vehicle) Shermans had arrived, and were soon distributed to front-line units, where British No. 19 radios were fitted and they were modified by the addition of sand shields and extra external storage.

That work was still in progress when the battle to drive the Germans back began at El Alamein on 23 October; but in all, 252 Sherman IIs and IIIs (M4A1s and diesel-powered M4A2s, we will recall) were battle-ready.

FIRST ACTION

It was shortly after sunrise on 24 October that the Sherman first went into action, when elements of the British 2nd Armoured Brigade met PzKpfw IIIs and IVs of the 15th Panzer Division. These were late-model German tanks, armed

Above: 'Napoleon', an early model M4 (note the suspension bogies) in support of British infantrymen in North Africa, late October, 1942. Shermans formed the spearhead of the British effort against the Axis.

with the long-barrelled 5cm and 7.5cm guns; the former were only marginally effective against the Shermans, but the latter were more than a match for the 75mm M3s. The British had a measure of surprise, however, and when they opened fire at 1800m (2000yds), they knocked out several Panzers. Then the German troops returned effective fire, disabling or destroying several Shermans in their turn before retreating northwards.

SHERMAN SPEARHEAD

From then on, the British Army's Shermans were to form the spearhead of the armoured thrusts which drove the Axis forces back pell-mell across Libya and into Tunisia, where, despite Rommel's brilliant rearguard action and massive reinforcement, they were trapped by Allied troops advancing

Above: An early M4 is seen here in training (note the covered bow machine gun). The three-piece differential cover, which is so prominent, was later replaced – though not in all types – by a single casting.

eastwards after the Operation Torch landings in Morocco and Algeria and were eventually forced to surrender in huge numbers.

SHORTCOMINGS AND STRENGTHS

It was in Tunisia that the Shermans first met the German 'super tanks,' a new generation of armoured vehicles – beginning with the PzKpfw VI Tiger – whose 8.8cm KwK 36 high-velocity guns were to cause them so much trouble in the future, particularly through France and Germany. But, initially at least, the untried American forces found the less-able PzKpfw IIIs and IVs, not to mention towed anti-tank guns manned by very experienced crews, difficult opponents, too: in the first combat between American and German troops, near Tebourba on 6 December 1942, for example, all five

Shermans deployed were knocked out without scoring significantly in return.

By that time, the Axis forces had faced up to the grim reality of the task which faced them in what was left of the territory they occupied in North Africa, and had begun a counter-offensive which was to cost the Allies, particularly the unexperienced Americans, dearly. It was in the battles which resulted, before the inevitable Axis capitulation in May 1943, that many US tank crews learned the hard lessons which were to turn them into such an effective force over the two years which were to follow. It was there, too, that many of the innate weaknesses of the Sherman's somewhat hurried design first showed up and were marked for elimination, though some shortcomings – notably the tank's poor turning circle, which resulted in inadequate performance on twisting mountain roads and in narrow village streets – never were to be addressed, except experimentally.

The tank had its strengths, too, of course: without them it would never have become the world-beater it was. It was in

discovering how to make use of these features that the American and British Sherman crews eventually became masters of the battlefield. Most important, perhaps, was the tanks' overall reliability, combined with relatively simple maintenance procedures, which allowed them to keep on going where lesser vehicles fell by the wayside; their low all-up weight and compact dimensions helped here too. In strategic terms this meant that the Sherman-equipped armoured divisions were ideally suited to long-range penetration (where the numbers available was also significant). In terms of combat tactics, the speed of their turrets' traverse and the accuracy of their gun control systems (as well as the stabilisation system fitted to the gun mount, which made firing on the move a practical possibility which it never was in the German tanks without it) was to make a telling difference – often that between success and failure – even though, as we have noted, there was no doubt of the clear superiority of the PzKpfw IVs' 7.5cm guns, let alone that of the longer, much improved version fitted to the Panther or the 8.8cm guns of the Tigers. Improved Shermans, fitted with the British 17-pounder gun, which could disable any German tank at all but the most extreme ranges, found the speed of traverse an even more telling advantage; it frequently resulted in them being able to knock out German heavy armour without even being shot at in return.

THE ITALY CAMPAIGN

Southern and Central Italy provides poor terrain for attacking tanks, as the Allies found out to their cost (though it must be said that the defending German forces sometimes had their difficulties, too, particularly in deploying heavy tanks in the abnormally wet weather of 1943) when they invaded after defeating the Axis forces in Africa. Here the heavy, better-armoured and yet, thanks to their regerative steering system, more manoeuvrable British Churchills often proved more effective than the Shermans, especially after local workshops started to cannibalise written-off Shermans for their M3 gun, which was then mounted in the Churchill turret in place of the original six-pounder. And by the time the Allies had broken through the German defensive lines

Left: A late-model M4A1, with cast hull, round-profile cast differential cover and loader's hatch, pictured here in Italy in 1944. Note the (strictly unofficial) *demigianna* of wine on the track guard!

Below: Soft road verges were a big problem in Northern France in 1944. This Sherman of the 12th Canadian Royal Tank Regiment (unit identifying symbols have been obscured by the censor) simply slid off the road.

and into the open country of the enormous Po Valley, where they had the advantage again, if only briefly, before committing to the Alps, their achievements were overshadowed by those of the units which had landed on the north and south coasts of France in the early summer of 1944.

THE PACIFIC THEATRE

By then, thanks to the availablity of more effective landing craft, the Sherman had been in action on the other side of the world for six months, in the Pacific theatre of operations, replacing the Light Tanks M3 which were all that was initially available to the US Marine Corps taking the brunt of the fighting for infantry support against the fanatical defending Japanese. By the time the Americans returned to the Philippines in 1944, the Shermans had become a regular part of the order of battle in independent battalions, their 75mm guns proving very effective against the prepared positions which were such a feature of Japanese defence, shooting the infantry in from medium and close range. Japanese armour – entirely ineffective against the American Mediums – was scarcely ever employed on the open battlefield, but usually

Below: M4 Shermans were deployed in the Pacific Theatre from mid-1943 onwards, in support of the US marines who bore the brunt of the fighting there. Many Shermans were equipped with flame weapons.

Above: The battle for the barren island of Iwo Jima, just eight square miles in extent, lasted six weeks and resulted in the virtual annihilation of the 21,000-strong Japanese garrison. M4s played a vital role.

served, dug well in and concealed, as auxiliary defensive strongpoints. Even with that advantage, it was no match for the Shermans and suffered badly. M4s supplied to the Chinese Nationalist forces, which operated alongside similarly equipped American tankers in Burma, played a more conventional infantry support role with equal success.

INVASION OF EUROPE

The lessons learned when the M4 first went into action in North Africa took some time to implement, but by the time the Allies were ready to invade Northern Europe, in mid-1944, improved models of Sherman were ready for issue, though the most significant improvement – the replacement of the M3 75mm gun by the M1/M1A1 76mm - was slow to be accepted.

The tanks were known as the Medium Tank M4 Series, Ultimate Design, though that was actually not to be the case; horizontal volute spring suspension and wide, centre-guided track, for example, was still to come. The reason usually given for their slow acceptance is the reluctance of armoured unit

commanders (right up to divisional level) to replace the tried-and-true 75mm gun with an unknown commodity on the eve of battle, and that must indeed have been a pervasive and persuasive argument, but given the marked superiority of the new weapon in tank-versus-tank fighting surely some greater effort should have been made to conquer this reluctance? (This superiority was not necessarily true in infantry support; it was widely held that the 75mm HE shell was better than the equivalent 76mm round.)

Unfortunately, there was no real opportunity to prove the new gun in combat before D-Day (Italy, as we have seen, was hardly an ideal battleground, and neither were the island jungles of the Pacific); it had not been available long enough in large numbers for a significant conventional training programme to have been established, and armoured force commanders simply wouldn't take the superiority of the 76mm gun on trust. As late as 12 June, almost a week after the invasion, firing demonstrations were still being held for senior officers who were still largely rejecting the tanks thus equipped – Patton, for example, said he would take an independent battalion 'on trial'.

They would change their minds most dramatically when the reality of fighting superior German tanks in the ideal defensive surroundings of the dense Normandy *bocage* was

Above: Laden with personal kit, this British M4A4/Sherman V makes its way inland from the coastal village of La Rivière in the period immediately after the Normandy landings, as infantrymen look on.

brought home to them later in the month, and were soon clamouring for all the 76mm-armed M4s they could lay their hands on.

The same reticence did not greet the introduction of the 105mm howitzer-armed version of the M4, largely because its role was perceived as being (and was) very different from that of the gun-armed tank.

The attrition rate amongst the Shermans in Normandy was high – it had always been imagined that it would be – but the situation was exacerbated by one particular feature of the terrain (though there was actually little excuse for the oversight; many areas of southern England, where the American armoured units mustered before the invasion, are similar in character): the narrow, twisty lanes and small fields were bounded by long-established hedgerows which provided excellent cover not only for enemy armour but also

for infantrymen armed with anti-tank weapons. In trying to negotiate the hedgerows and the earth banks upon which they are rooted, the tanks reared up and exposed their frail belly armour, which caused the demise of not a few.

THE SHERMANS' FINEST HOUR

As is often the case, the remedy was simple, however, and it fell to Sgt Curtis G. Culin of the 102nd Cavalry Reconnaissance Squadron to come up with it: a tusk-like arrangement of scrap iron, welded to the nose of the tank, low down on the final drive cover, that protruded in front of the track run and lodged in the base of the hedgerow bank. This prevented the tank from climbing and caused it, instead, to push out a section of the hedgerow, earth bank and all, interring any would-be ambusher in the process. Gen. Omar Bradley, to whom the Rhinoceros, as the device was rather predictably called, was demonstrated, was enthusiastic, and by the time the breakout from Normandy came, on 25 July, some 500 Shermans had been equipped with the devices, constructed of metal from German beach obstacles. (Sgt Culin was fittingly appointed to the Legion of Merit.)

The almost 10 months of fighting in Europe which followed were certainly the Sherman's finest period, even though by the end of a long career it was to have seen service in virtually every corner of the globe, in all sorts of terrain and climatic conditions. Available now in huge numbers, and enjoying the sort of air superiority armoured force commanders dream about, the US and British armoured divisions, strengthened by the Free French, who also received Shermans in significant numbers, were able to implement the sort of tactics the Panzer divisions they faced had themselves pioneered five years earlier: forcing through weak spots to fan out behind enemy lines, isolating pockets of strong opposition to be dealt with at a more convenient time and by more appropriate weapons, and cutting lines of communication and resupply.

The advance was checked briefly in the closed terrain of the hills and forests of the Ardennes, in eastern Belgium, at

Below: This M4A3, its tracks blown off by a mine, was an early casualty of the D-Day landings. Omaha beach, seen here, was, like the others, littered with the wreckage of destroyed and damaged vehicles.

Above: The advance across Northern France and into Belgium in the second half of 1944 was spearheaded by Sherman tanks. Note the 'duckbill' track extenders, fitted to lower the ground pressure.

Christmas, where the Shermans found themselves robbed of their ability to fight a manoeuvre battle and where instead they had to meet the Wehrmacht and SS Panzers head-on. Here, the tank destroyer variants, particularly the M36 with its superior 90mm gun, came to the fore. The partial and temporary German success during what came to be known as the Battle of the Bulge was helped on considerably by bad weather, which both prevented the US armoured forces from getting off the main roads to out-flank the enemy and from receiving much-needed resupplies of ammunition and fuel, but when the weather finally broke, so did the counter-attack, and from that point on there was little to stop the Allied tanks save for natural obstacles like the Rhine.

SIGNS OF VULNERABILITY

It is perhaps just as well that the defending forces the advancing Allies encountered were running desperately short of materièl, however, for by now the M4 was beginning to show its vulnerability; not only was it very clear that the M3 gun was just insufficiently powerful to allow them to fight the German heavy armour on anything like equal terms, but their own armour, too, was proving deficient, both against the Panzers' cannon and against the infantry anti-tank

weapons they were encountering in ever-increasing numbers.

In an effort to defeat the former, M4 crews added their own expedient armour wherever they could, often using plate cut from disabled enemy tanks, roughly welded into place (they used spare track shoes and roadwheels too, though these were markedly less effective). The latter, and particularly the heavier Panzerfaust 60, which could penetrate up to 200mm (nearly 8in) of plate, thanks to its shaped-charge warhead, was more difficult to defeat, and crews added sandbags, logs and even, occasionally, a coating of cement to their tanks in the attempt to stop them. This, in turn, led to reductions in both mobility and reliability, thanks to the extra weight. This time, the former was tackled, albeit with only limited success, by adding track extenders or 'grousers', but the latter was more difficult. Increased maintenance, particularly of the suspension units, paid dividends, but it was not until the arrival of tanks with the new horizontal volute spring suspension and the much wider centre-

Above: Shermans bore the brunt of the fighting during the German winter 1944 offensive in Belgium, the Battle of the Bulge, and eventually won through. This tanks is negotiating a forest road near Bastogne.

guide track that the problems were finally solved. Tanks thus equipped also came, in the main, with 76mm guns, and that, too, made a considerable difference to combat performance. Nonetheless, the American-standard Shermans still never came close to equalling the offensive power of the British-modified tanks with their 17-pounder guns, and if one has to single out a marque of Sherman as the best of its class overall, then the accolade certainly goes to the Firefly, cramped though its turret might have been, and its armour ultimately deficient.

AS GOOD AS THE T-34?

Was the Sherman as good an all-round tank as the other main contender for the dubious title of 'Best Allied Armoured Vehicle', the Soviet T-34/85? The Red Army, which got over 4000 Shermans, 2073 of them 76mm-gunned tanks, as part of Lend-Lease, didn't think so, but that says little or nothing about the real comparative merits of the two, for the T-34 was conceived specifically for the sort of conditions to be found in European Russia, and the Sherman was not. When the two types met in combat, in Korea, they proved to be quite well matched; the better ballistic performance of the Russian 85mm gun was effectively cancelled out by the speed with which an experienced Sherman turret crew could train and fire the stabilised 76mm gun of the M4; there was little difference in the effectiveness of the two tanks' armour.

KOREA

It was in Korea that the M4 Sherman went to war for the second time. When the North Korean Army attacked, on the morning of 25 June 1950, it was reminiscent of events in France just a decade earlier. There was little the defending forces in the south could do but run for cover, until eventually a defensive perimeter was established around Pusan in the very south. It was this bastion that the US Army, which formed the bulk of the UN-sponsored force sent to the peninsula, reinforced, and here that the armoured force of over 500 Medium tanks was concentrated. This included one battalion of the brand-new M46 Patton; the rest were M26 Pershings, introduced right at the very end of the European war, and late-model M4 Shermans, in about equal numbers. These tanks were the spearhead of the force which broke out of the Pusan perimeter in late September, and drove

Above: By the time of the so-called Suez War in 1956, the Israeli Defence Force had come to rely on the Sherman. The harsh conditions in Sinai meant that forward maintenance bases had to be established.

across the old North-South border, the 38th Parallel, not stopping until they came to the frontier with Manchuria.

It was during that drive north that the bulk of tank-versus-tank combat against the North Korean T-34s took place; when Communist China entered the war near the year's end, such battles virtually ceased, for the Chinese had very little armour. Instead, the M4s and M26s found themselves the targets of artillery fire and attacks by mases of infantry armed with lightweight anti-tank weapons and satchel charges. This was largely ineffective, and when the Chinese offensive, which had driven the UN forces back south, was at first halted and then reversed in February 1951, once again it was the US Army's Mediums which ruled the battlefield. After the armistice in 1953, Shermans continued to be employed in 'peace-keeping' duties until declared obsolete by the US Army in 1956.

ISRAELI WARS

The Sherman's combat career was far from over, however; that same year it went to war yet again, this time in the hands of the Israeli Army, but we have to backtrack a little way, to the earlier War of Independence the new Jewish state fought to establish itself in 1948, to trace the fuller history of the M4 in the Middle East. In the years immediately following 1948,

the Israeli Defence Force, Irgun ha-Haganah, with few outright friends anywhere, obtained its weaponry from diverse sources. Such tanks as it was able to lay hands on came largely from scrap-metal dealers in Italy; one source suggests that three intact Shermans were obtained clandestinely from the departing British but there is no evidence from contemporary Israeli sources to substantiate that. It does seem, though, that a single derelict British tank, one of a number scheduled to be scrapped by the simple expedient of taking them up Mount Carmel and pushing them off a cliff, was obtained with the connivance of British soldiers. This tank's engine was unserviceable, and it was without its gun, tracks and bogies; this was usually the case with the tanks obtained from Italy, too. The tracks had often simply been removed on site and were lying close at hand, or could be obtained from 'war surplus' dealers, but the guns (and gunsights) were much more difficult to replace; nonetheless, slowly, platoon by platoon, the IDF built its first armoured brigade, and one battalion of it consisted of salvaged Shermans (the rest of its vehicles were mostly French

Hotchkiss light tanks, but included two British Cromwells, brought over by deserters).

By the time of the Sinai War of 1956, the international climate had changed considerably, and Israel had been able to obtain surplus Shermans from the American government. These were M4A1s and M4A3s, fitted either with 76mm M1A2 guns or with obsolete 75mm M3s. The M3s were often replaced with French 75mm L/62 high-velocity guns, as developed for the revolutionary AMX 13, and probably the best gun of its calibre in the world at the time, fitted into re-jigged turrets with considerable modification to both the front plate and the rear, where a sizeable counter-weight reminiscent of that fitted to the M10 and M36 tank destroyers was mounted. Tanks thus modified were known as M50s or Super Shermans, and were very effective indeed against the likes of ex-Soviet T-34/85s in Egyptian hands. It was with these vehicles in the Sinai that the Israelis' reputation as some of the best tankers in the world was founded

Below: The Israeli Defence Force was almost entirely mechanised by 1956, its infantrymen going into battle in armoured personnel carriers behind a spearhead of Sherman tanks.

After the Sinai/Suez campaign, the IDF found itself in high regard amongst its allies in that ill-favoured venture, Britain and France. One result was a supply of much more effective British Centurion tanks, with their L7 105mm L/51 guns, which largely relegated the Israeli Shermans to reserve status. Largely, but not quite; there were still M4s in the Israeli ranks during the Six Days War of 1967, some of them with L/51 105mm guns somehow stuffed into the Phase Two turret which had originally housed the very much smaller and lighter 76mm M1A2 (this was in emulation of the French, also major users of the M4, who had first carried out this transformation on tanks of their own). These tanks, known as M51s, were usually re-engined, too, with Cummins VT8-460 diesels, which gave them an extended range and slightly higher top speed. With their new guns, they often succeeded in knocking out Soviet-built T-54s and T-55s, which were a whole generation ahead of them. Against all the odds, some of these tanks were still in service when Israel was forced to go to war yet again, in 1973, where they came up against T-62s and still won out, on occasion, three decades after the original Sherman had first seen action not above a few hundred miles away at El Alamein.

CHAPTER 4

The Sherman Variants

There were more variants of the M4 Sherman tank – and more diversity of them – than of any other armoured vehicle, before or since. They ranged from other varieties of frontline combat vehicles, like tank destroyers and flame-thrower tanks, to mine exploders, recovery tractors and armoured personnel carriers, and the Sherman chassis also formed the basis for a range of self-propelled guns and artillery pieces.

Many of the more bizarre variants, intended to perform more-or-less particular tasks during the assault on the invasion beaches, were devised in the UK, rather than in the USA, and in fact, the US Army shunned some of them. This programme was led by Major-General Sir Percy Hobart, and the resultant vehicles became known generically as 'Hobart's Funnies'; they were not exclusively Sherman-based: Churchill tanks were employed too. Some never made it past the prototype stage and some fairly promising developments were simply dropped at the war's end, when the requirement for them vanished, but others went on to be accepted weapons and support vehicles of modern mechanised warfare. The M4 Sherman was itself a development of the M3 Grant, of course; thus, many of the Sherman variants were originally based on the redundant M3 chassis, and may be regarded equally as having been M3 variants, though by the time most reached production, the lessons learned in the Sherman programme had been completely absorbed, and most are better seen as Sherman- than as Grant- based vehicles.

'TANKDOZERS' AND ARMOURED ENGINEERING VEHICLES
Perhaps the simplest of the modifications converted the standard gun-tank into an armoured bulldozer, capable of

Left: A Sherman DD takes to the water from a Landing Craft, Tank – the most dangerous part of the amphibious operation. During the Normandy landings, many were swamped before they reached the beaches.

clearing roadways, filling craters and the like while under fire. The modification was first proposed in January 1942 (though a number of tanks had previously been fitted with V-shaped blades at the Desert Warfare Center in California, and tried out for use in mine clearing operations) and experimental work continued, with little sense of urgency, it would appear, throughout that year, conducted by the Engineer Board of the US Army in conjunction with two manufacturers of regular bulldozer blades. Funds for the project were actually cut off in June 1943, but the two commercial concerns brought their development work to fruition anyway, and the blades they produced were fitted to a pair of Shermans. They were clearly very effective indeed, and procurement of the Bulldozer, Tank Mounting, M1, incorporating the best elements from the two designs, was immediately authorised. A total of 1957 complete kits were furnished by the war's end.

The M1 bulldozer, which had a blade 3150mm (124in) wide, was constructed for models of the tank fitted with the original vertical volute spring suspension and narrow tracks. It was mounted on a pair of support arms, which were in turn mounted on the centre suspension bogies, and the position and inclination of the blade was controlled by a hydraulic ram which acted between the tank's nose and the top of the blade. Later, a version for tanks fitted with HVSS suspension and wide tracks, with a 3505mm (138in) blade, was developed, which could also be fitted to the vertical-spring tanks with spaced suspension. This was designated the M1A1. Early in 1945, a mounting was produced which was independent of the tank's suspension, but which was fixed instead onto the upper hull front plate; this could be fitted with blades of varying width. It was designated the Bulldozer, Tank Mounting, M2.

IMPROVISED BULLDOZERS

In addition, bulldozer blades and mountings for them were sometimes improvised and fabricated locally; one particularly successful instance involved the tanks thus modified to fight ammunition fires (by the simple expedient of piling sand and earth on them) on the crowded Anzio beachead after the landings there in January 1944. Later, more specialised Sherman-derived vehicles specifically equipped to fight dangerous fires were developed at Fort Belvoir, Virginia. They had 5670l (1250 Imp gal/1500 US gal) internal water tanks and twin nozzles, which could be rotated through 180 degrees and elevated and depressed through a

Right: A Sherman tankdozer M1 of the US Army's 104th Division crossing the Treadway floating bridge across the River Ruhr, in February 1945.

60-degree range, fed by a 1900l (417 Imp gal/500 US gal) per minute capacity pump driven by an eight-cylinder, 85bhp engine. Additionally, a 567l- (125 Imp gal/150 US gal-) tank filled with a foaming solution was carried on the rear deck. These vehicles were sealed against blast, and 16mm (.63in) of additional armour was applied to the floor for added protection.

Tankdozers were used extensively in amphibious landings in the Pacific Theater of Operations, and 16 were assigned to Operation Overlord, the assault on the Normandy beaches, but unfortunately 10 of the latter were lost before they could get ashore, and of the remaining six, one was only able to make the beach by jettisoning its blade. Combat engineers were severely hampered by their loss. In more recent times, armoured engineering vehicles, rather than straightforward combat tanks, have become those equipped with bulldozer blades, but a number of modern main battle tank are equipped with such a device as standard.

TETHERED BOMBS

The prospect of being able to place or deliver weighty demolition charges from the relative security of an armoured vehicle was a seductive one, and attracted considerable

attention. The bulk of the effort expended in trying to come up with a workable method was concentrated on rockets with substantial warheads, but one other scheme stands out, if only by reason of it apparently being rather hare-brained. The tethered rocket-propelled 115kg (253lb) bomb was to have been towed 15m (50ft) behind the tank on an armoured trailer, to within a like distance of its objective. Its rocket motor would then have been ignited, causing it to fly in a semi-circular trajectory at the end of its tether, stabilised by a pair of 610mm (24in) square vertical fins, up and over the tank and down onto the target, where it would detonate. It was proposed that each trailer have space for six bombs, three with hollow-charge warheads for use against bunkers and hardened defensive installations, the other three with incendiary, fragmentation or conventional HE warheads. Tests carried out at the Ballistics Laboratory demonstrated that the weapon was actually effective, and could be delivered with considerable accuracy, but it was fairly low down on the priority list, and the tethered bomb was never developed fully.

DEMOLITION ROCKETS

As we noted above, the multiple rocket launchers were not suitable for the purpose of placing demolition charges, though the general principle worked well enough. Since the armoured engineering vehicles were to be used in the very forefront of the battle, they could expect to take sustained machine gun fire, to which the T64 launcher, a somewhat spindly gantry mounted above the turret, and consequently very exposed, proved vulnerable even though lightly armoured. In its place, it was resolved that a single-tube, breech-loading launcher which would fit into the Sherman's gun shield should be developed, and, in fact, two types, the T76 and the T105, both in 183mm calibre, were tried and found to be more-or-less successful, though neither was developed fully before the war's end. A more ambitious scheme to develop a rocket-armed demolition tank was also eventually still-born. The T31, as it was known, was based on an HVSS M4A3 chassis. It was armed with a pair of T94 183mm rocket launchers in armoured blisters, one each side of the (much narrower than normal) turret. These launchers were essentially revolvers, with five chambers in their cylinders; the chambers could be replenished from inside the tank, and it was envisaged that a minimum of 30 rockets would be carried. The turret had a dummy 105mm howitzer barrel, flanked by a pair of (very real) .30in machine guns. A vision cupola as fitted to the later M4 gun-tanks was fitted, as was a pedestal mount for a .50in anti-aircraft machine gun. The normal bow gun was retained, and the armament was completed by a flame-thrower in the right-hand sponson and a smaller version which could be fitted in either the bow gunner's or commander's position, in place of the periscope. The rocket launchers failed to operate properly in tests at Aberdeen (which were not carried out until August 1945),

and the project, though promising, was eventually cancelled early in 1947.

British combat engineering units converted many older Shermans to carry fascines (bundles of wooden stakes, each up to about 100mm (4in) in diameter; the bundles themselves were anything up to three metres (10ft) in diameter), which were used to fill anti-tank ditches, just as they had been employed at the first really successful armoured assault, at Cambrai in November 1917. The conversion was crude but effective: the turret was removed, and the aperture plated over, then a sloping tubular framework was constructed on the tank's deck. The fascine was hauled up and secured at the top, and could be released, to roll down and off in front of the tank, from inside the vehicle. Other, similarly neutralised vehicles were equipped with portable bridges, either folding types to be launched into position over a ditch or stream, or shorter structures which were fixed rigidly to the deck, in which case the entire vehicle would be driven into the ditch and left there until a more permanent structure could be put in place. US armoured forces experimented with similarly modified tanks, but not until 1945, and they never formed part of the regular Table of Organisation as they did in the British Army.

MINE CLEARANCE AND MINE EXPLODERS

Another part of the combat engineer's job – and a very hazardous part indeed – is the detection, clearance and neutralisation of mines, which by the start of World War II had

Above: A Sherman Crab I flail tank coming ashore at Walcheren Island, in the Scheldt Estuary near Antwerp, in November 1944, as part of Operation Infatuate, a seaborne landing which helped secure the port.

become one of the principal means of static defence, and here, clearly, the tank could be of very great assistance. Considerable ingenuity was applied to devising modifications to the tank which were at one and the same time simple, safe and sure, though looking at some of them, one could be perhaps forgiven for thinking that the first of those elements was sometimes overlooked. Basically, the choice was to either lift the mines, or detonate them ahead of the tank, and the second method had two sub-sets, one of which employed applying weight to them, the other setting them off either sympathetically or by blast, by means of explosives. Much of the research and development effort undertaken in the United States during the war was to be wasted, either through having taken a wrong turning (often very early on) or because the war finished before the device in question could be perfected (but of course, there is every reason to believe that America's capacity to devote considerable effort and large amounts of money to programmes which had only a small chance of success was one of the reasons that the Allies won World War II at all). In almost all cases, the venerable Sherman, which was as close as the Allies came to having a universal tank, was the vehicle chosen to mount the new equipment, be it operational or still only experimental.

Lifting mines by hand is a hazardous business in its own right, and the danger is increased many-fold when the task has to be carried out under fire; under the right circumstances it can be carried out mechanically, though, by excavation with a plough of some sort, and experimenters on both sides of the Atlantic (the British were the first to initiate a research programme as early as 1937) wasted no time in trying to come up with a successful design. There were to be the best part of a dozen different types of mine plough devised for the Sherman, either directly, or by modifying existing devices already in use with other tanks.

MINE EXCAVATORS

Mine excavators fall into two basic categories – those with snowplough-type mouldboards, and those which turn the earth over, like a farm implement. The best of the latter were probably the British Bullshorn and the MD1 ploughs, with a share mounted on a framework ahead of each track. The earth-turner type could be folded back over the tank's hull when not required, which improved its transportability. Both types were fitted to both Shermans and to Churchills; the

Below: A Sherman Crab I flails its way ashore during training. Note the breather tubes attached to the air inlet and exhaust, and the depth scale painted on the hull side. When not flailing, it functioned normally.

latter was not used operationally, though the Bullshorn plough was employed by elements of the British 79th Armoured Division (where it had been designed; the horn in question was to be found on the head of the bull which formed the division's insignia) on the Normandy beaches and in the dunes above them.

More complicated were the Farmer series, also developed in the UK. Three versions were produced, two of which used tines, rather than shares, to plough through the earth ahead of the tank, the Farmer Front covering the whole width of the vehicle, the Farmer Track covering only that portion where its tracks would run. The last, the Farmer Deck, used shares preceded by heavy rollers, intended to prevent them from digging in. Once again, they were fitted experimentally to both Shermans and Churchills, but were found to be unreliable.

Snowplough-like devices were certainly simpler, though they had a major drawback: they tended to carry with them a considerable quantity of earth, and thus occasionally buried mines more deeply instead of turning them up. The remedy for this was to fit the blades with long curved or wedge-shaped tines across their lower edges, and this worked to a degree, particularly in sand or light soil. The first US-developed blade plough, the T4, was straight and mounted diagonally across the vehicle. It was unsatisfactory, and instead two models with V-shaped blades, the T5 and T6,

Sherman variants

Above: The Sherman Crab's flailing chains beat the ground in front of the tank, seting off any mines secreted there, while the toothed discs on the extremeties of the shaft served as wire cutters.

Below: A Duplex Drive Sherman with its swimming screen in the stowed position. The bow machine gun was obscured, which reduced the tank's tactical efficiency; this drew considerable criticism.

Above: The Crocodile flamethrower stored its highly inflamable 'ammunition' in an armoured trailer, and was more popular with crews as a result. A few Shermans were converted to Crocodiles.

Below: Some Shermans were fitted with dozer blades, which were attached to the centre bogie each side and worked hydraulically from the M4's power traverse.

Above: The first flame weapons fitted to Shermans were ancilliary to the main armament, but later developments saw the main gun replaced by a flame tube.

were produced; the tops of their blades were curved over quite radically, in an attempt to prevent excavated mines from being carried up and over the blade – another perennial problem. Eventually the best points of modified T5 and T6 ploughs were combined into the T5E2 and T5E3. These were approved for limited procurement in June 1944, and 100 were produced and delivered between March and May 1945, and saw service in the Pacific against the Japanese. Updated versions of the V-bladed plough were subsequently introduced for the tanks which were to succeed the Sherman in service, and similar devices are still in use today.

MINE ROLLERS

Most of the mine detonators developed for the Sherman were in the form of rollers, to be pushed ahead of the tank. They were of two basic forms: very heavy, substantial items, intended to clear a path through a minefield, and much lighter devices, meant only to detect mines without significant loss of men or matériel, but only at the expense of a damaged or destroyed roller. A rather more sophisticated

form of the latter, the Lulu, used three lightweight wooden drums mounted on wooden beams as its rollers, two pushed ahead of the tank before the tracks, the third pulled along behind and between the tracks. Each drum housed an electrical coil which was sensitive to the metallic mass of a mine and triggered a loud buzzer when it passed over one (though actually, any body of ferrous metal would serve, and battlefields are notorious for the amount of scrap iron they contain). Once a mine (or a lump of scrap iron) had been detected, the operation halted until a sapper could come up on foot and dig it up, and if it was a mine, dispose of it; naturally, the man in question was very vulnerable, and this weakness put an end to Lulu's career.

The first of the exploder-detectors was the British AMRCR (Anti-Mine Reconnaissance Castor Roller), developed for the Sherman V. AMRCR consisted of four independently sprung castor rollers (that is, rollers with an axle carried on a yoke which was itself located on a vertical pin), mounted in tandem pairs ahead of each track, on arms bolted to the first and second suspension bogies. Like most mine rollers, these were fabricated from steel plate discs, this time in two different diameters, and assembled so that the smaller acted as spacers. Each one was the width of the early pattern track. The AMRCR-equipped tank drove slowly through the suspect area until it detonated a mine and then retired along its own track to allow flail-equipped tanks (qv) to come in and deal with the menace, jettisoning the arms (which were held on by explosive bolts) if necessary. The device worked after a fashion, but was very clumsy to manoeuvre and comparatively expensive for something which was of its nature disposable. It, too, fell by the wayside.

An attempt was made in Canada to make the device more durable, by the expedient of loosely mounting the vertical pins which carried the rollers on a cross-bar which linked the two arms, so that if a mine exploded under one, it would be thrown up and around the bar, a spade on the yoke digging in and lifting the arm on that side up so that the roller could pass underneath, back to the trailing position. This became known as the Canadian Indestructible Roller Device (CIRD), and was made in two versions, with 394mm- (15.5in-) wide and 635mm- (25in-) diameter and 457mm- (18in-) wide and 711mm- (28in-) diameter rollers (which were in this case forged from the solid; each one weighed over a tonne). CIRD Shermans were issued on a one-per-troop basis to flail tank-equipped units in northwestern Europe, from the time of the invasion until the end of 1944, but were also used in conjunction with other mine clearing devices such as the explosive-filled hose known as Tapeworm (see below).

Much larger and heavier roller assemblies were also constructed, designed this time not simply to detect the presence of a minefield by detonating a single mine, but actually to clear a path through it. The first American experiments centred on the M3 tank fitted with the Mine Exploder, T1, – an assemblage of three rollers, two pushed ahead of the tank, in front of the tracks, the third pulled behind. Each roller was 1020mm (40in) in diameter, and the front pair were composed of four disks assembled with spacers on an axle, the rear with five. Trials showed that the device had considerable potential, and a second version, T1E1, was made up and demonstrated on 10 December 1943 mounted on a prototype, Sherman-derived M32 Tank Recovery Vehicle

Below: US Marines, faced with defenders protected within deep-set concrete bunkers, favoured flame weapons above all other forms of offensive weapon.

(qv). Now all three rollers were mounted in front of the vehicle, and the crane jib, which was attached to the sponsons at the level of the top of the inclined front glacis plate, was rigged so that they could be lifted out of the crater a detonating mine would cause. Each roller was now composed of six 1220mm- (48in-) diameter disks, 50mm (2in) thick, loosely mounted with spacers between them, and the whole ensemble weighed 16.4 tonnes (16.1 tons). Some 75 were produced during April 1944.

The device, nicknamed Earthworm, was very effective at detonating mines and proved to be indestructible, but it was very difficult to manoeuvre at the best of times, and impossible in mud or over rough ground. In an attempt to improve on that, the centre roller was deleted, and the remaining pair were increased in diameter to 1830mm (72in), reduced in thickness to 37mm (1.5in) and increased in number to seven. In an attempt to keep the weight down, they were pierced with eight large holes, and the ensemble, now known as the T1E2 weighed 12.75 tonnes (12.5 tons), and cleared a pair of tracks just over 1020mm (40in) wide. It was to grow in size still further.

'AUNT JEMIMA'

In its next version, as the T1E3, the discs were 2440mm (96in) in diameter and 70mm (2.75in) thick, and five together made up a roller. The most significant difference, however, was the development of a rudimentary chain drive, which worked off external auxiliary sprockets on the track drive sprockets, which meant that the rollers were steerable to a degree. The complete unit now weighed close to 27.25 tonnes (26.8 tons), and cleared twin paths 864mm (34in) wide. Two hundred were manufactured in all, between March and December 1944. They were known to the troops as 'Aunt Jemima', and some were in use in France by the time of the break-out operation from the Normandy beachhead in June 1944, and again around the Atlantic port of Brest, and in the east between Nancy and Metz. In September 1944 two US tank battalions, the 738th and 739th, which had previously operated CDL searchlight tanks (see below) were converted to mine-clearing formations, and by the following month each was equipped with 18 T1E1s, 24 T1E3s and 12 tankdozers.

The final evolution of this arrangement was the T1E5, which had slightly smaller rollers with serrated edges. Being considerably lighter than the T1E3, it was somewhat more manoeuvrable. Rather better in this respect was a basically similar device produced by Chrysler, which had a single roller the full width of the tank's hull, made up of 16 serrated discs, 1220mm (48in) in diameter carried in an inverted cradle and attached at the centre of its front edge to a pair of curved booms which ran over the top of it, to be fixed to the sponson sides just aft of the drive sprockets. A second version, extended by the addition of three extra discs, was produced for tanks with HVSS suspension and wide tracks.

T1E4s and T1E6s were produced in limited numbers during 1945.

Perhaps the most bizarre of all the roller-type mine exploders was the still-born T10, made from a converted M4A2 by Fisher by removing the tracks and suspension units, cutting back the sponsons at the front and fitting two 2440mm (96in) rollers where the drive sprockets had been. Each of these rollers was just over 915mm (36in) wide, and the gap between them was covered by a third 1830mm- (72in-) wide trailing roller. The ground clearance of the vehicle was 1400mm (55in), and it weighed in at 53 tonnes (52 tons). Its operating speed was just over three kilometres per hour (two miles per hour) and it could attain a maximum of about three times that on the road. Just one prototype was constructed and tested in June 1944 before the project was cancelled.

FLAILS

The T1 series were the best of the roller-type mine exploders, but even as the T1E1 was going into limited production, an alternative was actually going into operation. First tried in the UK in the pre-war period but never developed, it consisted of an array of chains fixed to a rotating boom which was driven by an auxiliary engine, which beat the ground ahead of the tank. The idea was revived in the summer of 1941 by a South African named du Toit, who built a lorry-mounted test rig and demonstrated it to Gen. Auchinleck, who recognised its potential at once. Du Toit referred to his device as a threshing machine, but early on, another related name was adopted instead and became generic: the flail.

The original flails, fitted to British Matilda tanks and used in action in North Africa in 1942, were effective to a degree, but were extremely temperamental (though that is hardly surprising: they were fabricated on the spot in regimental workshops by men who had only the haziest notion of what they were doing, and without anything in the way of a formal research and development process; it is more surprising that they worked at all). These Matilda Scorpions, as they were known, became the prototypes for the entire genre. They were soon rendered obsolete when a full-scale development programme began in the UK, and when the front-drive Grant and Sherman tanks arrived (the British Matildas and the Valentines, to which Scorpion flails were also fitted, were rear-drive) they were immediately co-opted, for the flails could be driven directly off their running gear, without the need for auxiliary motors. A prototype was completed in May 1943, but proved to be full of flaws. Meanwhile, the original auxiliary powered Scorpion had crossed the Atlantic, and appeared on a converted M4A4, which was tested at Aberdeen. It was successful enough that Pressed Steel Car Co was asked to produce 30 conversion kits in April 1943 (and 11 more in the following July), and the T3 Sherman Scorpions saw action in the break-out from Anzio before being superseded by a direct-drive version, the T3E1. From that time on, the flail mine exploder became standard equipment in the Allied armies, AEC Ltd in the UK (where virtually all British development work was carried out) having produced a lighter, much more reliable version known as the Crab, 300 of which were ordered for delivery in time for the invasion of France.

EXPLOSIVE DEVICES

As we have already noted, there was an alternative to applying a heavy roller or beating the ground. Instead, pressure could be brought to bear on buried mines by means of a controlled explosion if only a satisfactory way of deploying a detonating charge could be found. The main German anti-tank mine, the Teller, with its 11kg (24lb) charge of TNT, was particularly susceptible to such a technique, and that encouraged development to proceed. To be practicable, explosive mine clearance has to be an area, rather than a point, operation, and by quite early on in World War II, two rival methods of deploying the charges had surfaced – one either launched bombs at the minefield in a linear pattern, or laid a line charge across it. By 1943, the British had developed their AVRE, which was fitted with a spigot mortar launcher for the Blacker Petard, better known to the men who used it as the 'Flying Dustbin', which carried a 12kg (26lb) charge of TNT, and used it successfully to blast a way through minefields, and similar devices were soon developed in the USA for mounting on Sherman tanks. The first was the Mine Exploder, T12 – a multiple spigot mortar capable of launching twenty-five 52kg (115lb) T13 bombs, which could be mounted on a Sherman with its turret removed. The spigots were arranged in rows, each one at a successively steeper angle (from about 45 degrees in front to about 80 degrees at the rear) and the combined weight of 1300kg (2875lb) of explosive could clear a path more than six metres (20ft) wide and 77m (250ft) long, starting from a point about 46m (150ft) in front of the launch vehicle. The charges detonated in the air (though only just), the fuse being located in a nose extension. Three pilot vehicles were converted and tested in mid-1944, but by that time, work which had gone on in parallel on the development of rocket-propelled charges seemed set to show better dividends, and the T12 spigot mortar was abandoned.

The rocket-propelled charge was much heavier – a 273mm (10.75in) T91 rocket which carried 110kg (240lb) of high-explosive. Launchers were deployed on an armoured trailer towed behind the tank, and the launching sequence was automatic; once initiated a new rocket was fired every six metres (20ft) and exploded on impact, some 18.5m (60ft) ahead of the tank. Trials showed some promise, and an operational version, the T59, with 30 launchers, was ordered, this time firing a round for every four and a half metres (15ft) of forward progress. The project was cancelled in August 1945 before the pilot was delivered.

Above: Schnorkel apparatus was developed for the various types of Sherman, which – together with a kit to seal all apertures – allowed them to wade up to the level of the turret top.

Line charges were to prove more successful ultimately, and are in widespread use today in a very similar form to that perfected by the war's end, but the early versions were either very difficult to manoeuvre, like Snake, or hazardous to deploy, like Tapeworm. Snake was a development of the Bangalore torpedo used for breaching wire entanglements since World War I, and was produced originally in Canada. It consisted of six-metre (20ft) lengths of pipe (some contemporary accounts called it drainpipe, others called it scaffolding tubes) filled with TNT, which were towed in bundles into the operational area, then joined together. The tank which had delivered them would then retreat to the back of the line, hook up a chain fixed to the two towing eyes on the

Above: The M3-derived Howitzer Motor Carriage M7 – this one is in action in Italy, early 1944 – was known as the Priest, thanks to the pulpit-like appearance of the defensive machine-gun installation.

transmission cover, and push the ensemble ahead of it into the minefield. A Sherman was able to propel a 122m (400ft) length of Snake, which weighed 7.15 tonnes (seven tons), of which almost a ton and a half was explosive. (A later version used oval-section tubing and upped the weight of the charge to two tons; later still, aluminium tubing was substituted, which reduced the all-up weight by two and a half tons.) It was detonated by firing one of the tank's machine guns at an impact-sensitive fuse located at the rear of the assembled tube. In the right conditions, Snake cleared a (very obvious) path 122m (400ft) long and six metres (20ft) wide.

Tapeworm was a 457m (1500ft) length of canvas firehose filled with plastic explosive (in all but the first 15m [50ft], which was filled with sand, to protect the towing tank from the blast). It was towed to the edge of the minefield in a trailer, and then hooked up to a Sherman fitted with CIRD, which deployed it across the minefield. This in itself was often a hazardous undertaking, and Tapeworm was not particularly popular as a result. More spectacular, certainly, was Conger. This device consisted of a Universal Carrier (a light, open-topped tracked vehicle which, as its name suggests, served as a maid-of-all-work in the British Army) loaded with 300m (330yds) of neoprene-impregnated canvas hose, a tank containing a liquid explosive derived from nitro-glycerine, bottles of compressed air and a 127mm (5in) rocket launcher. The carrier was towed to the edge of the minefield by a Sherman, and the rocket launcher used to shoot the hosepipe into place. It was then filled with explosive using the compressed air, and detonated – if it hadn't gone off by itself already, a distressingly frequent occurrence. Conger was used in Normandy and on into Germany, but few of the men who deployed it ever trusted it. More recently, the introduction of inert explosives has made the process safe and reliable, and successors to Conger (known as MICLIC, for MIne Clearing LIne Charge, to the US Army and Giant Viper to the British), are in current use.

THE DRAGON M1

Despite the inherently dangerous nature of the device, the US Army thought enough of it to develop versions of its own, based on an M10 gun carrier derived from the Sherman tank. The Dragon M1, as it was known, carried 152m (490ft) of hose and a ton of desensitised nitroglycerine, which it deployed in a similar way to Conger. A second version, Dragon M2, was based on a stripped-out Sherman, with its crew reduced to three. They deployed three lengths of hosepipe in parallel, some two to two and a half metres (seven to eight feet) apart, before filling them from a two-ton tank of liquid explosive; this was necessary to clear a sufficiently wide path through Japanese anti-tank mines, which were not as sensitive as their German counterparts. A much less volatile version of the Dragon, the Projected Line Charge, M1, used plastic explosive moulded around a nylon rope and covered with a knitted sleeve, tied to the rope every 152mm (6in), which gave it the appearance of an enormous string of sausages. These line charges were also deployed by rocket launcher, but in shorter lengths. They were packed on wooden pallets and towed to the edge of the minefield by a standard Sherman, where they were turned over to combat engineers.

A variety of ways of modifying Sherman to deploy mine clearing explosive charges as they advanced were also developed. The best was probably Pancake, which had a pair of seven metre (22ft) -long armoured conveyor belts mounted, one each side of the tank, angled up so that their leading ends were 3.35m (11ft) above the ground. These conveyors were fed through holes cut in the sponsons with shaped charges consisting of 6.8kg (15lb) of TNT with a command wire attached. When they reached the end of the line, they dropped off, were briefly arrested just above ground level by the command wire, and then detonated. The stripped-out tank had space to stow 150 of these charges, which was reckoned to be enough to clear a path 245m (803ft) long. Pancake was successfully demonstrated in February 1945, but was judged to be inferior to both the Snake and the T59 multiple rocket launcher.

The wastage rate of tanks in combat can be very high indeed, but by no means all are total losses or are even actually damaged, as opposed to having broken down. Originally, other tanks were used to tow disabled vehicles off

THE MINE-PROOF TANK

The majority of the Sherman-based mine clearing devices never got past the prototype phase, and neither did the supposedly mine-proof tank, chiefly because it was not what it set out to be. The original Mine Exploder, T14, was a reworked early M4, with its belly armour thickened and modified running gear. Trials at Aberdeen showed that much more work was necessary, and a late-model was now modified to become the T15, with much heavier cast armour welded to the floor pan and forged roadwheels, partially protected by plate armour shields which extended down from the sponson sides. The turret was removed and replaced by a 25mm (one inch) sheet of flat rolled armour, fitted with a vision cupola and a small oval hatch. The only mechanical modification involved the fitting of the 3.36:1 final drive from an M4A3E2, and the 33.2-tonne (32.6-ton) vehicle could attain around 29kmh (18mph) as a result. A second version with heavier suspension components and much heavier track shoes became the T15E1. Plans were also drawn up for a T15E2, with 50mm (two inches) of extra belly armour, to be spring-mounted, but the vehicle was never built. Test at Aberdeen proved that the vehicles were still vulnerable to heavy anti-tank mines, but nonetheless, further development was contemplated; it was halted by the war's end.

the battlefield, but they were rarely adequate for the job. By 1942, the US Army had begun to experiment with converting medium tanks to the role of prime movers for artillery pieces (see below) with only limited success, but it was clear that they had a future as tank recovery vehicles (TRVs), and in late September 1942 the order was given to convert 750 M3s. Later, M3A3s and M3A5s (with the siamese-twin GMC 6046 diesel engine) were also employed. These first generation TRVs were designated as T2s, and were later standardised as M31s (with the suffixes -B1 and -B2 added to differentiate between the three versions); they were essentially similar save that the power take-off for the double jaw-type winch was via the transmission of the air-cooled petrol engine and direct from the diesels, which necessitated detail changes in the way their superstructures were laid out. They were equipped with a crane jib which was anchored where the 37mm turret had been (a dummy turret front, with a dummy gun, was fitted; a dummy 75mm gun replaced the original, too, and was mounted in a concealed access door), with a pair of boom jacks, the feet of which were located at the very rear of the vehicle (when the jib could lift 4.55 tonnes [4.46 tons]) for travelling, but which could also be deployed on the ground, when the safe working load was tripled. The winch cable could be led directly out of the vehicle to the front or rear, or it could be taken over a sheave on the jib head. The winch capacity was 27.3 tonnes (26.8 tons). The M31s retained the bow machine gun, and a second, de-mountable M1919 gun was supplied, to be mounted on a traversing ring in the fake turret.

In March 1943 it was recognised that the number of M3s available for conversion was limited, and that operating them alongside M4 combat tanks created logistical difficulties. The following month the Ordnance Committee authorised the conversion of M4s of all types to become T5 TRVs, with a simple fixed turret welded from rolled plate, fitted with a .50in machine gun on a traversing ring. An 81mm mortar was mounted on the hull front (and was meant chiefly for launching smoke bombs) and the original bow machine gun was retained. The crane jib now became a simple A-frame, anchored at the points where the front deck met the glacis plate and supported at the rear by a much smaller A-frame anchored at the rear of the rear deck. This was the normal travelling position, and was also used for elevated towing, but the jib could also be deployed forwards. A version with the turret deleted entirely was also tested, as the T7, but was found to be inferior. The T5 was standardised as the M32 early in June 1943, with -B suffixes to differentiate between

the various hull/powerplant combinations. Over 1500 were manufactured before the end of World War II, together with over 800 M3-based recovery vehicles, and later, more M4s were converted to this role as the rather more capable still M74. The British Army used converted Canadian Rams and M3 Grants, but also produced its own conversions of the Sherman, the ARV I and II.

A variant of the ARV was developed especially to operate on the beaches of northern Europe, intended to tow stranded vehicles out of the surf during amphibious operations. The BARV was fitted with a box-like metal superstructure which allowed it to operate in up to three metres (ten feet) of water, and the crew included a trained diver, whose job it was to fix the towing cable. Around fifty were produced, and some stayed in British service until well after the war was over.

PRIME MOVERS, CARGO AND PERSONNEL CARRIERS

Some of the early tank recovery vehicles – M3-derived M31s and M4A1-derived M32B1s – were later converted to prime movers for the artillery, by removing turrets, booms winches and armament, and a similar conversion was later performed on more than 200 M10A1 three-inch Gun Motor Carriages (see below), which were themselves derived from M4A3 gun-tanks. They were fitted with compressors to provide air at high pressure for the guns' and howitzers' braking systems, but were otherwise unmodified. They were designated as M33, M34 and M35 respectively, and a total of just

Above: A British Sherman-based 155mm Gun Motor Carriage in Italy in the summer of 1944.

Left: Some Canadian Ram tanks had their turrets removed and were thus transformed into Armoured Personnel Carriers. In this form they were known as Kangaroos.

under 350 were produced. The M30 cargo carriers were significantly different, being based on the M12 self-propelled gun chassis which was derived from that of the M3 tank but with the powerplant moved forward, to a position just behind the driving compartment (see below). This same arrangement was adopted for the cargo carrier, to leave a clear load space at the rear, where it was intended that 40 rounds of 155mm ammunition could be stowed. When the upgraded T83/M40 SPG was conceived, in 1944, it used the late-model Sherman hull (from the M4A3), with HVSS suspension and wide track, and a small number of cargo carriers were built to the same specification.

The increasingly close coordination between infantry and armour which was the hallmark of Allied tactics in north-western Europe dictated that the foot-soldiers be provided with transport capable of keeping up with the tanks and protecting them when they came under fire. The solution

A LESSON IGNORED

The failure to break out from the beaches of Dieppe during the disastrous Operation Jubilee in August 1942 brought home the need for an armoured engineering tractor to spearhead the clearing of obstacles during amphibious operations. In the UK, Churchill tanks were modified into Armoured Vehicles, Royal Engineers (AVREs) with considerable success (thanks not least to their large physical size and ample interior) and in February 1943 the US Army Corps of Engineers requested that a similar project be undertaken in the USA. A test site near the Amphibious Training Base at Fort Pierce, Florida, was selected, and after six months of experimentation, approval was given for the trial conversion of a few Shermans. The first, an M4A3, had its gun removed and a pair of 25mm- (1in-) thick doors set in its place. Its ammunition storage racks were taken out, and a second access door was cut in the right sponson, between the middle and rear bogies. Hand rails and a rear step were welded on, and an M1 bulldozer blade mounting was fitted. Lastly, an experimental 20-tube launcher for 190mm (7.5in) rockets, designated the T2, was mounted on arms above the turret.

It was soon concluded that the doors set in the turret face would be both inconvenient and highly danger-ous to use while in action, and that the introduction of a very weak spot right at the most vulnerable location in the tank would be little short of disastrous. A subsequent pilot conversion had the cannon removed and replaced by a steel plug, but the mount and shield (together with the elevating gear) were left in place. Instead, a second side door was fitted, in the left- hand sponson, slightly ahead of the middle bogie. This tank was fitted with the T64 multiple rocket launcher (a version of the T40/M17, see below), which had very much longer rails; a pivoted arm linked it with the gun shield, so that it could be elevated and depressed (tests later revealed the inherent weakness of this device in this context, and it was replaced; see below. Conventional tanks were also fitted with multiple rocket launchers for use in the bombardment role, rather than for demolition or to lay a covering smokescreen, as it was intended they be employed in the armoured engineering vehicle, and we shall return to that subject too).

As initially conceived, the armoured engineering vehicle was to be little more than a means of getting combat engineers into position to place their charges by hand, and it was to have carried an operating crew of two and a four-man demolition team, together with 454kg (1000lb) of plastic explosive in the turret basket and further supplies in the right-hand sponson and below the turret floor. The basic plan was for three of the engineers to dismount and place charges while the fourth passed them out. A range of acces-sories were tested along with the converted tanks themselves; they included an armoured trailer carrying a further ton of explosives and a variety of sleds to achieve the same end, and a means of placing charges carried on the 'dozer blade.

The trials of the new vehicle went very slowly, and were in no way hastened by the attitude of the US military hierarchy, which could not agree within itself just how these new vehicles were to be distributed and where they would fit within the Table of Organisation. As a result (though perhaps only partially), although the conversion of a total of 100 tanks was eventually sanctioned, only two had actually been completed by the time the war ended – and they got no further than the port of embarkation. This was in direct contrast to their British allies, who by D-Day had three regiments, each equipped with 60 AVREs, organised into the 1st Assault Brigade, Royal Engineers. To the end, US sappers were forced to try to attain their objectives on their own two feet, carrying just a man-load of satchel charges, while their British colleagues were working more effectively from the shelter of their justifiably popular modified Churchills.

was to utilise modified tank hulls, and it seems that the first units to be so equipped were elements of the Canadian 2nd Corps, who stripped the guns and ammunition storage racks out of M7 Priest gun carriages (see below) and used them during Operation Totalize (the Canadian component of the break-out from Normandy) in August 1944. Priests were in short supply, however, and a better solution was found in the Ram tanks, brought over to the UK for training purposes, but now largely redundant (in fact, the early Rams, with their small auxiliary turret, were ideal for the purpose, since the machine gun mounted there could give fire support to the infantrymen as they de-bussed; late-model Rams, which lacked the turret, got machine guns mounted on the turret ring instead). The tanks' main turrets were removed, along with most of their interior fittings, and in this form they could carry a (reduced) section of eight infantrymen, plus

Above: The British converted all available Sherman models to the Firefly configuration – this is an M4A1, which the British called the Sherman I, adding the suffix 'C' to denote its up-gunned status.

their drivers and a machine gunner. More than 200 Rams were converted in this way, and the Kangeroos, as they were called, were used to equip two regiments, one British and one Canadian, assigned to the 79th Armoured Division. Additional Kangeroos were produced locally, particularly in Italy, from redundant Priests and Sextons and early-production Shermans. They were often employed to tow 17-pounder anti-tank guns into action, too.

AMPHIBIOUS SHERMANS

Proposals for methods of converting tanks into amphibious (or fully submersible) vehicles were common enough in the late 1930s, the latter gaining some favour in the Soviet Union – and amongst Germans, who expected to have to fight there – as a means of crossing rivers. The alternative to traversing a river – or the sometimes treacherous stretch of sea between landing craft and beach – by simply driving across on the bottom was to persuade a tank to float, and one of the pioneers in this field was a Hungarian named Nicholas Straussler, who immigrated into Britain in the late 1930s, and who had also been involved in early experiments with mine ploughs. Straussler experimented successfully enough with floats on a variety of light armoured vehicles, but had to admit defeat when it came to heavier, cruiser tanks, for the dimensions of the floats themselves became so great that the law of diminishing returns began to take effect.

Straussler's insight was to realise that not just closed chambers but open-topped objects – boats, or buckets, for example – float, and that the same principle could be applied to a tank by the simple expedient of fitting it with what amounted to a huge collapsible watertight tube, sealed to its hull at the bottom and open at the top, which could be erected so that the volume of air it contained compensated for the mass of the tank beneath. This floatation screen could be erected before the tank took to the water (from riverbank or landing craft) by pumping air into inflatable ribs (which were reinforced by a collapsible framework of steel tubing), and quickly let down after it had emerged on the beach or the far bank. The only significant requirement on the part of the tank was for its gun's barrel not to protrude beyond the hull front, but that could be satisfied by simply elevating it, and there was a concomitant drawback in that the gun could not be fired with the screen erected (and the bow machine gun was obscured even when it was lowered).

AMPHIBIOUS SHERMANS

The first effective amphibious tanks produced by this method were Valentines, but the design really came into its own when it was modified to suit the Sherman. One of the most important modifications was to dispense with the power take-off from the engine, which Straussler had originally employed, and drive the propellers by way of the tracks instead. Special sprocket plates were attached to the idler wheels, which meshed with the track shoes and located with a pair of bevel gears and pinions, which in turn drove the paired 660mm (26in) contra-rotating propellers. The propellers could be oriented either manually or hydraulically to steer the tank in the water, and gave a top speed of perhaps five knots (10kmh [six miles per hour]). They were turned up through 90 degrees when not in use, and held by a pair of latches which could be released remotely to allow them to fall into the operating position, where they were held by their own weight and the pressure of their rotation. This alternative second method of supplying motive power gave the system its name: Duplex Drive, or DD.

The floatation screens provided ample freeboard – 1235mm (48.63in) in front and 925mm (36.42in) behind in a Sherman V (M4A4), with its lengthened hull; slightly less with the Sherman III (M4A2). A bilge pump was fitted, as were periscope extensions and a small platform, welded to the right-rear of the turret, where a helmsman could stand. The only substantial drawbacks were the screen obscuring the bow machine gun, even when it was lowered, and its vulnerability to even fairly light projectiles below the waterline – several Sherman DDs were lost on D-Day as a result of mortar and small-arms fire, but many more were lost by simple swamping in the higher-than-predicted swells.

In all, three regiments of British Sherman DDs were employed on D-Day in Normandy, as well as two more from Canada and three US Army tank battalions, the 70th, 741st and 743rd (though the 741st lost 27 of its 29 tanks through swamping, a most unusually high toll). DDs were also employed in the landings on the south coast of France. They were subsequently used in river-crossing operations throughout the rest of the campaign in northwest Europe, the last time they were employed being on 29 April 1945, during an assault crossing of the Elbe by a squadron of the Staffordshire Yeomanry. Early on, there were instances of DDs being unable to haul themselves up steep, muddy riverbanks, and some tanks were fitted with rocket boosters to give them a helping shove, though there is no evidence that any such device was ever used in combat. Straussler himself also developed an aid to landing – a folded mat mounted on a framework high above the tank's bow, which was projected in front of the vehicle by compressed air and then de-coupled, and up which it and following tanks then climbed. Known for some reason as 'Ginandit' (any resemblance to a Martini cocktail being completely invisible to this author), development continued for some months after the war's end, but there is no evidence to suggest that it was ever used in combat, either.

Some influential senior men in the US Army didn't like the Straussler modification for the simple and quite good reason that its armament could not be fired while the tank was in the water, and they were very critical, too, of its seaworthiness, particularly after the 741st's disastrous experience. In due course alternative means of enabling the tank to swim were developed, the most successful of which, the T6, used specially fabricated steel buoyancy chambers, compartmentalised and filled with plastic foam, attached to the front rear and sides. Even though the foremost and rearmost sections of the longitudinal floats could be up when the tank was in transit, the device still took up a great deal of space, being almost 14.5m (48ft) long. Tanks thus equipped were propelled by their tracks, and had a maximum speed of perhaps five kilometres per hour (three miles per hour), which was certainly not enough to allow them to make headway against a falling tide, but they were used with some limited degree of success in the Pacific, right at the end of the war against Japan, though it was judged that simple preparation for deep fording – rendering all the openings in the hull watertight, and fitting schnorkels – was more effective; this permitted the tank to operate normally in about two metres (6.5ft) of water. Nonetheless, a total of 500 of the conversion kits were manufactured, and it was standardised as the Floatation Device, M19. Another, similar, floatation device consisted of a pair of standard 15.24-tonne (15-ton) capacity engineers' pontoons, fixed one each side of the tank and fitted with outboard motors, was also tested, and was accepted as a 'field expedient' solution. Alternatively, two amphibious DUKWs could be attached to the M4, one each side, and this gave enough buoyancy to float the tank. This method was approved for short river-crossings, but certainly wasn't practical in combat.

Right: The Gun Motor Carriage M10 came about as a result of the success of fitting a 105mm howitzer on the medium tank chassis. The M10 had an open-topped, low-sloped turret.

The notion of mounting searchlights with 'shaped' beams inside tank turrets originated in France in the 1930s, and was taken up by both the British and American armies, who adapted M3 tanks – which were well fitted, for once, to the task, by virtue of their main armament not being mounted in a centre-line turret – in fairly large numbers. The searchlight employed a mirror which was parabolic in the vertical plane and elliptical in the horizontal plane, and thus produced a beam which was much wider than it was high – at a range of 900m (1000yds) it subtended 305m (1000ft) horizontally and just 32m (105ft) vertically. Its light source was a carbon arc lamp of 13,000,000 candlepower and it could be obscured by a motor-driven metal shutter operating at two different speeds to produce a dizzying stroboscopic effect as well as providing normal illumination. It was powered by a 10Kw generator, driven off the main powerplant. The project became known as the Canal Defence Light in an effort to hide its real purpose, and this veil of secrecy was its undoing – so secure was it that no field-level commanders knew of its existence or capabilities, and none were prepared to send it into action as a result, even though (according to one knowledgeable source) no less than 1850 M3s were converted to the CDL specification in the UK alone (and almost 500 more were produced in the USA). By November 1944, when Allied armour losses were beginning to tell, the majority of CDL units had still seen no action, and could no longer be spared;

the searchlights were de-mounted, and their tanks reconverted to other purposes – mine explosion was the most important. A small number were retained, and were extremely useful during the Rhine crossings.

A NEW TURRET

Efforts aimed at converting Shermans to the CDL specification – which required an entirely new turret – began in mid-1943, and prototypes based on the M4, with twin lights and but a single ball-mounted .30in machine gun in the turret, were tested in mid-1944, one in the USA and two in the UK. A vehicle with just one searchlight and a lightweight 75mm M6 cannon, was also constructed in the United States. It was completed in January 1945, trials were concluded six months later, and it was universally accepted as being a very effective weapon – but once again, the war was to be over in both theatres before the next step could be taken, and the project was shelved. Five years later it was briefly revived, and plans were drawn up to fit the turret to a late-production M4A3 HVSS hull, but a simple calculation showed that four entire medium tank battalions could be equipped with standard 457mm (18in) searchlights for the cost of just one

Below: The Gun Motor Carriage M10 was an effective tank destroyer, particularly when fitted with the British 17-pounder gun, which was also used to equip the Sherman Firefly.

new CDL tank, and therefore the project was finally scrapped for good.

American experiments with flame-thrower tanks began with the Medium Tank, M2, but soon shifted over to the much more suitable M3, which could mount a flame gun in its turret and still retain its main armament. Both gas-pressurised and pump-pressurised systems were tested, but neither was immediately successful, the former, which used raw gasoline as its fuel, had an effective range of no more than 32m (105ft), and the latter, which used thickened fuel, was not effective at all. Efforts then shifted over to mounting the man-portable M1A1 flame-thrower on the Light Tank, M3, and this had some limited success, though the Canadian Ronson flame gun proved much more effective, and was used with considerable success in the Pacific theater.

FLAME-THROWERS

The first time an M4 was employed in combat with an effective flame-gun was on the island of Guam on 22 July 1944 when six M4A2s of the US Marine Corps went into action with E5 flame-guns replacing their bow machine guns. The gas-pressurised guns, which used gasoline thickened with four and a half per cent Napalm (a combination of naphthenic and palmitic acids, and akin to liquid soap) had a combat range of some 60m (1970ft) at a working pressure of around 24.5kg/sq cm (350psi). Performance was severely limited by the small amount of fuel which the tank could carry – just 90l (20 Imp gal/24 US gal) in a tank in the right sponson, and sometimes another smaller tank mounted above the transmission between driver and bow gunner – and still retain its main armament ammunition storage capacity. Other auxiliary flame-throwers were developed which could be located in place of one or other of the M6 periscope mounts, either in the bow gunner's hatch or in the turret roof. Their range and limitations were much the same as those of the E5, as were those of a unit manufactured locally (in Hawaii) which was mounted alongside the bow machine gun. These auxiliary devices were never particularly popular with tank crews, but they were in service right to the end of the war against Japan because they were so effective in reducing hardened defensive installations hidden in the jungle.

More popular and more effective were the main-armament flame-throwers – modified Ronsons initially, mounted in salvaged 75mm gun tubes – fed from four tanks with a total capacity of 1100l (240 Imp gal/290 US gal) in the hull floor, below the (shortened) turret basket. The pressurisation agent this time was carbon dioxide in place of compressed air, and was stored in liquid form in the right-hand sponson and heated to bring it to the gaseous state at 21kg/sq cm (300psi). The fuel used was now six per cent Napalm, and the effective range was similar to that achieved with the E5. Eight M4A3s were converted and issued to the 4th and 5th Marine Divisions in time for the assault on Iwo

Jima on 19 February 1945, where they proved very effective indeed. A much larger force of M4 flame-throwers – 54 in all – supported the US Army on Okinawa during the three months of heavy fighting there.

Meanwhile, back in the United States, a development programme for a main armament flame-gun had got underway in the summer of 1943, and some 12 months later one version, the E12-7R1, was authorised for limited production for mounting in M4A1 or M4A3 turrets, in a shroud designed to look like a 75mm gun tube. The fuel capacity was 10 per cent greater than that of the vehicles produced in Hawaii, and the effective range, using nitrogen- or air-pressurised eight per cent Napalm, was almost doubled, to around 115m (125yds). Construction started in November 1944 and the initial order – for just 20 tanks – was completed in April 1945, by which time further production had been ordered. In all, some 640 of the units, by now standardised as the M5-4, were authorised for production, but only just over 150 had actually been manufactured by the time the war ended. The tanks armed with them were redesignated as the M42B1 and -B3 respectively, but none saw combat in World War II. Other projects to develop flame-guns were also authorised, one from a commercial company, the others from Massachusetts Institute of Technology and the University of Iowa. All three produced satisfactory results, but none was put into production. Even then, the story was not finished, for after the end of the war, flame-systems for Sherman tanks continued to be developed, the last of them leading to the testing of the turretless T68 Self-propelled flame-thrower at the end of 1953.

THE CROCODILE

The British had also initiated a development programme for flame weapons, amongst the most successful of which was Crocodile, with its fuel tanks and pressurisation system housed in an armoured trailer, to be towed behind a Churchill, or later a Cromwell, tank. A US Army team saw a demonstration of the Churchill Crocodile in March 1943, and promptly ordered 100 units, adapted for fitting to Sherman tanks, with a further 25 as spares, but the production process was delayed, and only four were actually delivered before the order was cancelled in August 1944. The four were issued anyway, to a platoon of the 739th Tank Battalion (which had previously been a CDL unit), which deployed them with great effect. The US Ninth Army promptly requested that the original order be reinstated, but the request was turned down for two reasons: British manufacturers had their hands full with orders for their own army, and there was a widespread belief that a US-produced system would soon be available.

British Shermans were also fitted with two very effective types of self-contained flame-weapons (that is, with the fuel tanks and pressurisation gear within the tank), the Salamander and the Adder, both of which used Wasp flame-guns, while the Canadian Army used the Ram tank with its turret removed and a Wasp flame-gun mounted in place of

Sherman variants

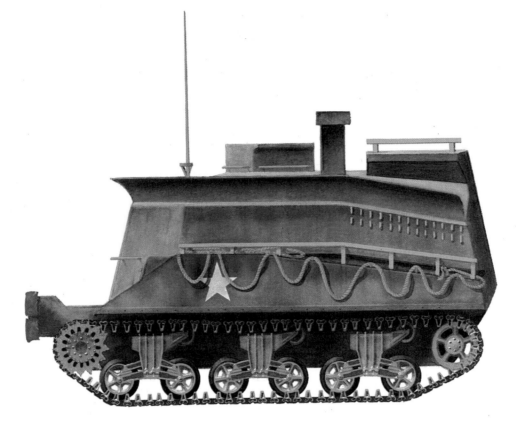

Above: The Beach Armoured Recovery Vehicle was produced in the UK, prior to the Normandy landings. Its (fixed) superstructure allowed it to operate in up to three metres (ten feet) of water.

Below: The Mine Resistant Vehicle T15E1 was an attempt to produce a tank capable of simply rolling through a minefield. An expensive development programme produced no useful results.

Above: The T-34 was an early attempt to produce a rocket bombardment weapon capable of surviving on the battlefield itself. It mounted sixty tubes, each loaded with a 4.5in rocket.

Below: "Aunt Jemima", as the T1E3 Mine Exploder device was nicknamed, saw limited service in Europe after D-Day. It was sometimes necessary to employ a second Sherman to push from behind.

the bow machine gun, which it called the Badger. Later, Shermans were converted to the same configuration. The Wasp guns had a range of between 75m and 90m (82-98.5yds), depending upon the type of pressurisation used. It was the tactical success of the Sherman Badger which inspired the programme that led to the development of the T68 in the USA.

ANTI-AIRCRAFT TANKS

The success of Hitler's blitzkrieg tactics, which used aircraft in the ground attack role to supplement traditional artillery, made it necessary to develop mobile anti-aircraft artillery (AAA) batteries to defend against the threat posed, in particular, to armoured columns, and it was obvious that the AAA vehicles would need to be compatible with the tanks they were to protect; thus, why not use the same chassis for both? When the self-propelled AAA development programme was begun in the USA in the autumn of 1941, the tank in question was the M3, of course, and once again, the first attempts at producing a variant used the M3 chassis.

Above: An M10 tank destroyer, armed with a 3in M7 gun, taking part in what amounts to an impromptu victory parade through an Italian city. Almost 5000 M10s were built, and a further 1700 improved M10Als.

Work began in November on a prototype known as the T26, with the M2 75mm gun (which had started life, we may recall, as an anti-aircraft gun anyway) in a high-elevation turret with all-round traverse and a sophisticated (for its day) fire control/prediction system, but it had not progressed very far when test results showed the gun to be unsuitable in the role, and it was discontinued. Instead, it was proposed to mount a 40mm quick-firing gun in its place, and this was designated the T36. Two were completed (very much behind schedule, thanks to problems with the fire control system) and operational testing took place over the winter. Modifications were made during the spring of 1943, and more testing took place, but it was fairly obvious that the single 40mm cannon provided insufficient firepower, and problems of access for maintenance, of ammunition stowage and with the fire control system proved insurmountable too. T36 was scrapped in July.

A revised specification suggesting either two 40mm guns or a singleton flanked by paired .50in machine guns had been put forward in May 1942, and a design for a mounting to hold the latter configuration was produced from an ostensibly rather unlikely quarter – the Firestone Tire and Rubber Co. This was approved, and the production of two prototypes for mounting on M4 tank chassis (M4A2s were used) was authorised in July. The turret in this case was a ball-type – that is, the guns were fixed in it and the whole unit both revolved in the turret ring and tilted on central trunnions. In practice, the two-man turret crew was hopelessly overworked, and there was no room to fit in a third man; ammunition storage was inadequate and spent cases from the machine guns tended to jam the traverse – which in any event was too slow to keep low-flying aircraft engaged in traverse. Some modifications were made in an attempt to satisfy the criticisms, but the result was not much more successful, and T52 in its turn was scrapped (but not, somewhat surprisingly, until the autumn of 1944).

ANTI-AIRCRAFT SHERMANS

The best self-propelled light anti-aircraft (AA) installation on the Sherman chassis – though it came too late to see the sort of action it was designed for – was actually Canadian; it employed quadruple Polsten 20mm cannon, in emulation of what was certainly the most successful such design of the war, the German *Flakvierling* 38, which first appeared in 1941 mounted on a half-track truck and was then transferred to the fully tracked PzKpfw IV in 1943. The Skink, as the Canadian AA tank was known, was built at the Montreal Locomotive Works on the hull of the M4A1, production starting in January 1945, by which time the Allied air forces in Europe had achieved marked air superiority and there was no real tactical need for it. As a result, just three complete vehicles, and turret/armament kits to convert five more, were built. Only one was ever used in combat, mostly against ground targets, where its high rate of fire (the guns could be fired singly, in pairs or all together, when its cyclical rate was something approaching 1600 rounds per minute) and HE/Incendiary ammunition proved devastating. In trials it proved just as effective against low-flying aircraft, and its redesigned turret traverse system, which could perform a complete rotation in six seconds, ensured that the criticism of the T52's poor performance against beam targets was not repeated.

We have noted that multiple rocket launcher installations proved ineffective when used in the demolition role aboard armoured engineering vehicles due to their susceptibility to machine gun and mortar fire, but in the area fire support role, where the vehicle carrying them wasn't required to go into the front line, they proved very satisfactory. The Rocket Launcher, T34, which was the first type fitted to M4-series

tanks, was a substantial device with a total of 60 launch tubes, 36 in a double row, and 24 in two double rows of 12 beneath. The array of 2286mm- (90in-) long plastic tubes was supported to the rear of the centre of balance by a pair of vertical arms fixed to the turret sides and at the front by a single arm fixed by means of a split-ring clamp to the gun tube, so that elevating the gun elevated the rocket launcher, too. This arrangement was found to be unsatisfactory in practice because the gun could not be fired until the launcher had been jettisoned (itself a less-than-straightforward operation), and later versions had the anterior support fixed to the gun shield, which cured the problem. The 115mm (4.5in) M8 rockets were fin-stabilised, though that actually did little enough to improve their accuracy. They were joined by rather better spin-stabilised M16 rockets in similar calibre during 1945, a new launcher, the T72, with 60 much shorter tubes being developed for it. They had a range of almost five kilometres (three miles). Short-range 115mm (4.5in) naval bombardment rockets were used by land forces too, the tubes of the T45 (Mark 7 to the US Navy) launchers mounted in two arrays, each side of the turret.

Another naval weapon, this time a rocket-powered anti-submarine depth charge, was the inspiration for a much heavier fin-stabilised 183mm (7.2in) rocket, the T37, intended primarily for demolition, which carried a warhead containing 14.5kg (32lb) of plastic explosive. For these rockets the 20-tube T40 launcher was developed, but as noted above, it proved vulnerable to heavy machine gun fire despite being completely enclosed in 12.7mm (.5in) armour plate. Nonetheless, it was standardised as the M17 and used with some success in the invasion of southern France (Operation Dragoon) and in the hard fighting through and beyond the Gothic Line in central Italy. A better-protected version, the T73, which held just 10 rockets in a single row, but which could be elevated independently of the tank's gun, was introduced right at the war's end.

GUN MOTOR CARRIAGES

It should be borne firmly in mind that the US Army's tactical doctrine for the use of armour was still evolving when World War II broke out in Europe in September 1939, and it was not really until late in 1941 that a clear picture of the requirements of modern warfare backed up by solid combat experience began to emerge. Just as it was clearly necessary to provide armoured divisions with anti-aircraft guns mounted on vehicles which could stay with the tanks wherever they went, so it was also clear they would have to be provided with artillery which could fulfil the same requirements, and to that end, plans to mount artillery pieces on the chassis of M3 tanks were drawn up. Two pilot vehicles, known as T32s, were produced by the Baldwin Locomotive Works, both of them mounting the M2A1 105mm howitzer (the same piece which would later find its way into the M4-series tanks) on the upper part of the standard field carriage just to the right of the centreline in the cut-down, open-topped superstructure, and with the driving position moved to the left. The first prototype was tested at Fort Knox in February 1942, and the T32 was soon approved for service with just a few minor modifications to the thickness and extent of the armour and, more crucially it was to turn out, to the disposition of the howitzer. The modifications – which included the provision of a mounting for a .50in AA machine gun, were made to the second pilot vehicle, which was then shipped to ALCO to serve as a production pattern. The T32 was standardised as the Howitzer Motor Carriage, M7 in April 1942, and the first two production versions were shipped to the Aberdeen Proving Grounds early in that month. The Priest, as the M7 became known to the British Army (because, it is said, of the pulpit-like appearance of the AA machine gun mount, which occupied roughly the position the 75mm gun took up in the original M3) was to stay in continuous production until August of the following year, by which time over 2800 had been produced. Very early production vehicles used the rivetted lower hull of the M3, but the vast majority of M7s had the welded lower hull of the M4, together with the second series suspension bogies, with their heavier-duty springs.

THE PRIEST IN ACTION

The Priest first saw action alongside the M4A1 at the Battle of El Alamein in October 1942, and by the end of the year – by which time the US Army's own armoured divisions had taken it into action in Tunisia – plans were being drawn up for an improved version incorporating many of the modifications which had been introduced into the M4 tanks (including the cast transmission/final drive cover), as well as changes to ammunition stowage to improve its levels of protection. Further production orders for almost 700 improved M7s were placed with ALCO and Federal Machine and Welder, which brought the total production to almost 3500. More than 800 more, based on the M4A3 and using the Ford GAA engine, were built at Pressed Steel Car Co as the M7B1. At no time was the HVSS suspension and widened track ever fitted.

Early on in the M7's combat career, in the mountainous terrain of Italy, a shortcoming of the howitzer's modified mounting had shown up. In order to reduce the vehicle's profile, it had been decided from the start to limit the tube's elevation to +35 degrees, which proved inadequate in indirect fire across the hills and ridges dividing one valley from another. The solution had been to bulldoze steep ramps to elevate the entire vehicle (an expedient which the howitzer-equipped M4 tanks were also to adopt in similar circumstances), but somewhat curiously, no attempt ever seems to have been made to correct the deficiency by returning the mounting to its original +65-degree elevation limit. It was not until almost a decade later, when the M7 went to war again in Korea, that the defect was made good, modified vehicles being designated M7B2s.

Having served as the production prototype for the M7, the second T32 was subsequently modified to carry the British 25-pounder gun, but at the same time, the Montreal Locomotive Works in Canada began work on a similar project based on the Ram, which showed more promise. The American project was cancelled, and early in 1943 the Canadian self-propelled 25-pounder went into production as the Sexton. Its gun was mounted to the left of the centre line, the driver being seated on the right of the vehicle in accordance with British practice, and the simple box-like superstructure was made up of welded armour plate, 12.7mm (.5in) thick on the sides and rear and 18.75mm (.75in) thick on the front face. Many of the improvements introduced into the Sherman chassis found their way into the Sexton – heavy-duty vertical volute springing and the cast, one-piece transmission cover, for example – and it soon became the British Army's standard self-propelled light artillery piece, replacing the Priests, which were converted to other purposes. A total of 2150 Sexton Is and IIs were produced, and continued in British and Canadian service long after World War II was over.

THE 155MM GMC M12 AND M40

There was little interest in developing self-propelled artillery in the USA or in the UK during the inter-war period, even though there had been some enthusiasm for the concept during the latter part of World War I. Interest revived in the United States in the summer of 1941 (a key period, of course, as we have seen), and alongside the T32 project a design was put forward for a much heavier motor carriage mounting a 155mm -calibre gun. Once again, the chassis chosen was that of the M3, while the gun was to be the apparently obsolescent M1917 or M1918, left over, as their designation indicates, from World War I. The design was dubbed the T6, and a prototype was constructed at the Rock Island Arsenal and delivered to Aberdeen in mid-February 1942. The only significant modification to the M3 chassis involved moving the powerplant to the front, to a position just behind the driver, and altering the form of the final drive cover to allow for the steeper angle of the propeller shaft. Even in its initial form, the T6 soon proved itself to be a stable gun platform, and its only serious defect was the design of the hydraulically actuated spade at the rear, which was dug into the ground to prevent the whole carriage from moving backwards under recoil. The spade was redesigned, and the modified carriage submitted for service testing at Fort Bragg where it soon proved itself to be most effective – in one test it fired from one position and then moved 10km (six miles) to a new location and commenced firing again in a 35-minute period, where a towed gun would have taken three hours or more to perform the same manoeuvre.

The Artillery Board suddenly became very enthusiastic about the project, and in mid-July recommended that the T6 be adopted, along with a purpose-built ammunition carrier based on the same modified M3 chassis, to be known as the T14. The T6 was subsequently standardised as the 155mm

Gun Motor Carriage M12 (and the T14 later became the M30), and 50 were ordered from Pressed Steel Car Co; that order was soon doubled, and the last batch of five vehicles was delivered in March 1943.

The M12 proved to be a very effective weapon indeed, and in the break out from the Normandy front in 1944 it often bore the brunt of the fire support task as 'conventional' towed artillery was left behind. When it came to attacking the Siegfried Line of defensive installations in the autumn, it was often used in the direct fire role, the 155mm rounds proving immediately effective against German pillboxes when fitted with concrete-piercing fuses, penetrating up to two metres (6.5ft) before exploding. The M12s were deployed to within 900m (1000yds) of the defensive line on some occasions, and the gun crews sometimes found themselves in hand-to-hand combat as a result. Indeed, so effective was it that the Artillery Board soon asked for more – a request which was impossible to fulfil since the limited supply of M1917/M1918 guns was now exhausted.

Planners had anticipated just such a demand, and as early as the spring of 1944 had set about devising a replacement. Originally it was intended simply to adapt the design to accept the new, more powerful M1 155mm gun, but it soon became evident that the M3-based M12 was simply not

Above: The Sherman-based 155mm Gun Motor Carriages were probably the most effective self-propelled artillery pieces of World War II, going on to see service in Korea.

strong enough, and a more comprehensive redesign, using late-production M4 chassis with HVSS and wide tracks, was put into effect. The T83, as the prototype was known, went for trial in July, and proved very satisfactory right from the start – and when the 155mm M1 was replaced with a 203mm M1 howitzer, it proved equal to that task, too. The T83 was standardised as the 155mm Motor Gun Carriage M40 in May 1945, over 400 being delivered before the year's end; 24 were converted to T89 specification, with the larger howitzer, and these were standardised as 203mm Motor Gun Carriage M43s in November, and a further two dozen were produced specifically.

Though the T83/T89 was introduced too late to see general service in World War II, one example of each, along with some M26 Pershing tanks and other newly developed pieces of ordnance, were rushed to Europe and sent into action as part of an evaluation exercise known as Zebra. The two new MGCs were allocated to the 991st Field Artillery Battalion (which promptly replaced the 203mm howitzer aboard the T89 with a 155mm M1 gun, in the interests of uniformity) and used in the bombardment of Cologne. The howitzer was later reinstated, and the T89 saw action in its original form, too. The two Sherman-based MGCs were to be the backbone of the US Army's self-propelled artillery assets in Korea. Experiments were conducted using the MGC as the basis for an even more devastating bombardment weapon, employing the 250mm mortar, but these came to nothing. A rather more practical plan to equip M4 tanks with 155mm breech-loading mortars was also cancelled.

THE M36 TANK DESTROYER

Even while the original M3 Grant concept was being finalised, proposals for a much lighter, more mobile version of what was basically the same vehicle were being put forward. These vehicles were to act as front line defensive elements – essentially, highly mobile anti-tank guns, with the offensive capability to knock out enemy armour, making up for their lack of protection with speed and agility. An experimental unit – the Tank Destroyer Center – was set up at Fort Meade, Maryland, on 1 December 1941, and its first task was to evaluate the first concrete proposal, that for the T24 – basically, a Medium Tank M3 chassis with its turret and sponson removed and an M3 76mm anti-aircraft gun mounted in its stead. The T24 used a standard anti-aircraft gun mount, and had a very high profile as a result. It was soon clear that this was unacceptable, and the prototype vehicle was sent off back to the Baldwin Locomotive Works, where the original modification had been carried out, for further development. The result was the T40, with its gun – an M1918 of the same calibre by this time – mounted lower down on a traversing ring, firing through a cut-out in the front of the superstructure. This was standardised as the 76mm M9 Gun Motor Carriage at the end of April 1942, though the project soon ground to a halt, largely because it turned out that only 27 M1918 guns were available, and that not all of them were serviceable!

In the meantime, a proposal to use the M4 chassis, its turret replaced by a much lighter unit open at the top and rear, and mounting a 76mm anti-aircraft gun, had also been put forward. The Gun Motor Carriage T35 dated from mid-November 1941, and a mock-up, based on the hull of a (diesel-engined) M4A2, with the 76mm T12 gun, was delivered the following January. In the original, the bow machine gun was retained, and the profile of the hull armour followed that of the tank, though it was reduced to 25mm (one inch) thick in all but the front plate. Further modifications were soon made following after-action reports from the fighting in the Philippines, and a lower silhouette, with more heavily angled armour, and without the bow gun, was put forward as the T35E1. Prototypes of both designs were ordered from Fisher and were delivered in April 1942.

The main difference, of course, was in the turret, which was both lighter and very much simpler than the original – a circular bin, essentially, cast in one piece (though the origi-

nal specification had called for it to be welded from rolled plate, and to be hexagonal in plan), sloping out from both top and bottom rings to a pronounced waist, with a partial roof covering the gun breech. Tests at Aberdeen showed that the sloping armour of the revised hull design was much more effective than the original, but that the cast turret was a poor substitute for the welded version. The decision was taken to revert to the original turret, and to reduce it in thickness to 37mm (1.5in) on the front plate and 18.75mm (.75in) on the upper sides, though manufacturing difficulties led to the design being modified before production, and a pentagonal turret being adopted. A one-piece cast differential and final drive cover was specified, and thus modified, the T35E1 was standardised as the Gun Motor Carriage M10 on 4 June 1942. Its gun was to be the 76mm Gun M7 in the M5 mount, which was itself modified so as to be able to accept the trunnion pins from either the 105mm howitzer or the British 17-pounder anti-tank gun, as later fitted to the Sherman Firefly; British M10s were thus modified, to become the Achilles, with outstanding success.

THE M10/ACHILLES

The M10 went into production at Fisher in September 1942; by December of the following year, a total of almost 5000 had been delivered, and, in addition, a version based on the M4A3, known as the M10A1, was also put into production, and a further 1700 were manufactured. In terms of performance, the M10 was really only marginally different from the M4A2 on which it was based; it was barely .53 tonnes (.5 tons) lighter (thanks, as much as anything, to the need to add 2.1 tonnes (two tons) of counter-weights to the rear of the turret, to balance the gun), its theoretical top speed was the same, and so were its endurance and agility. If it had any major factor in its favour, it was probably cost and time-in-production, while its maintenance was somewhat simplified in the field. For the three-man turret crew, its main advantage over the 'senior' version was probably the speed with which one could abandon it, *in extremis*.

As early as the spring of 1942, the M10's 76mm gun was beginning to look distinctly impotent in the face of newly improved German armour, and a project to up-gun the tank destroyer was set in train. The weapon chosen was another which had started life as an anti-aircraft gun: the 90mm T7, and early trials indicated that there would be no untoward problems in employing it. In fact, it was to be November, 1943 before the first production orders for what were then designated T71s were placed, the delay being due to 'minor' modifications turning into a thorough redesign of the turret. The new vehicle was standardised in July 1944 as the 90mm Gun Motor Carriage M36, and it soon proved very popular with its crews and the infantry it supported alike; in the M36 gun, American troops at last had a weapon able to stand up against the Tigers and Panthers, the best tanks the Germans could field.

Medium Tank M4A3 'General Sherman' — Specification

Crew	Five
Hull length	6.22m (20.4ft)
Length, gun forward	6.22m (20.4ft)
Width, without sandshields	2.62m (8.6ft)
Height, to hatch top	2.74m (9ft)
Transportation weight	28.35 tonnes (27.8 tons)
Combat weight	30.26 tonnes (29.72 tons)
Ground pressure	0.96kg sq cm (13.7psi)
Ground clearance	0.43m (1.42ft)
Fording depth, without preparation	0.91m (3.0ft)
Fording depth, prepared	Amphibious
Maximum gradient	60 per cent
Maximum trench crossing	2.29m (7.5ft)
Maximum step climbing	0.61m (2ft)

Suspension type	Volute-sprung bogies
Number of bogies	Three per side
Roadwheels per bogie	Two
Return rollers	Three per side
Wheel size	508 x 229mm (20 x 9in)
Tyres	Rubber

Powerplant type	Ford GAA petrol
Configuration	Four-stroke V-8 @ 60 degrees; DOHC per bank
Valves	Two per cylinder
Material	Cast-iron crankcase and block; cast-iron heads
Nominal output	500hp @ 2600rpm
Nominal efficiency	36hp/litre
Power/weight ratio (combat)	16.5hp/tonne
Capacity	1100 cu in (18,020cc)
Bore	137mm (5.4in)
Stroke	152.4mm (6in)
Compression ratio	7.5:1
Aspiration	Two four-choke carburettors
Crankshaft bearings	Five
Lubrication system	Wet sump
Oil capacity	121 litres (8 US gallons/26.5 Imp gallons)
Coolant type	Liquid, fan-assisted
Fuel capacity	635 litres (168 US gallons/139.7 Imp gallons)
Nominal range, road	210km (130 miles)
Nominal range, cross-country	130km (80 miles)
Nominal maximum speed	42km/h (26mph)
Transmission type	Manual, five forward one reverse
Final drive	Herringbone gear
Driven sprocket	Front

Gear ratios
1st	7.56:1 4km/h (2.5mph)
2nd	3.11:1 9.8km/h (6.1mph)
3rd	1.78:1 17.2km/h (10.7mph)
4th	1.11:1 27.5km/h (17.1mph)
5th	0.73:1 41.8km/h (26mph)
Reverse	5.65:1 5.5km/h (3.4mph)
Final drive ratio	2.84:1

Steering type	Lever-controlled differential
Minimum turning radius	9.45m (31ft)

Main armament	L/37.5 75mm Gun, M3 in Mount M34A1
Secondary armament	Two .30in M1919A4 machine guns; one co-axially mounted, one hull mounted
Ancilliary armament	One .50in M2 AA machine gun
	One 2in Mortar, M3
	One .45in M1928A1 SMG
	.45in M1911 pistols
Main armament ammunition	97 rounds
Secondary armament ammunition	4750 rounds
Ancilliary armament ammunition	300 rounds/.50in
	600 rounds/.45in
	12 2in Mortar rounds
	12 hand grenades

Armour	Rolled homogenous nickel-steel plate; cast nickel-steel turret (dimensions are nominal)
Hull front	51mm (2in)
Hull side	38mm (1.5in)
Hull rear	38mm (1.5in)
Hull top	19mm (.75in)
Hull bottom	12.7-25.5mm (.5-1in)
Turret front	76mm (3in)
Gun shield	88mm (3.5in)
Rotor shield	51mm (2in)
Turret sides	51mm (2in)
Turret rear	51mm (2in)
Turret top	25.5mm (1in)

Turret traverse method	Electrical
Traverse rate	24 degrees per second
Elevation method	Manual
Elevation range	Plus 25 to minus 10 degrees

The Sherman's Main Rivals

VEHICLE	PZKPFW PANTHER AUSF. G	T34 - 76A	CROMWELL MK V
Crew	Five	Four	Five
Hull length	6.95m (22.75ft)	6.1m (20ft)	6.24m (20.47ft)
Length, gun forward	8.85m (29ft)	6.1m (20ft)	6.4m (21ft)
Width	3.25m (10.7ft)	3.0m (9.84ft)	3.05m (10ft)
Height (to hatch)	3m (9.85ft)	2.45m (8ft)	2.46m (8ft)
Weight	45.5 tonnes (44.7 tons)	26.5 tonnes (26 tons)	27.9 tonnes (27.45 tons)
Ground pressure (kg sq cm)	0.75	0.64	0.95
Fording capacity	1.9m (6.2ft)	1.1m (3.6ft)	0.9/1.22m (2.95/4ft)
Gradient	70 per cent	70 per cent	47 per cent
Trench	2.45m (8ft)	3.0m (9.84ft)	2.3m (7.54ft)
Step	0.9m (2.95ft)	0.9m (2.95ft)	0.9m (2.95ft)
Suspension type	Torsion bars	Christie/coil springs	Christie/coil springs
Powerplant	HL230 P30 V-12 petrol	V-2-34 V-12 diesel	R-R Meteor V-12 petrol
Output	700hp	500hp	600hp
Power/weight ratio	15.5hp/tonne	19hp/tonne	21.5hp/tonne
Capacity	23,095cc	38,900cc	26,900cc
Fuel capacity	730 litres (193 gallons US)	420 litres (111 gallons US)	525 litres (138 gallons US)
Range, road	200km (120 miles)	450km (281 miles)	280km (175 miles)
Range, cross-country	100km (60 miles)	260km (162.5 miles)	
Nominal maximun speed	55km/h (34.5mph)	47kmph (29.37mph)	62kmph (38.75mph)
Steering type	Single-radius regenerative	Clutches	Regenerative
Turning radius	4.35m (14.3ft)	3.8m (12.46ft)	In place
Main armament	7.5cm L/70 KwK42	76.2mm L/30.5 M1938	75mm L36.5 Mk V
Secondary armament	Two 7.92mm MG34 MG	Two 7.62mm DT MG	Two 7.92mm Besa MG
Main armament ammunition	82 rounds	80 rounds	64 rounds (composite)
Secondary ammunition	4800 rounds	2400 rounds	4952 rounds
Armour	Rolled, welded	Rolled, welded	Rolled, welded/riveted
Hull front	50-80mm (2-3.1in)	45mm (1.77in)	63mm (2.48in)
Hull sides	40-50mm (1.57-2in)	45mm (1.77in)	32mm (1.26in)
Hull rear	40mm (1.57in)	40mm (1.57in)	32mm (1.26in)
Hull top	16mm (.65in)	20mm (.78in)	20mm (.78in)
Hull bottom	16mm (.65in)	15mm (.59in)	14mm (.55in)
Turret front	100mm (3.95in)	45mm (1.77in)	76mm (2.3in)
Mantlet	120mm (4.75in)	–	–
Turret sides	45mm (1.77in)	45mm (1.77in)	63mm (2.48in)
Turret rear	45mm (1.77in)	40mm (1.57in)	57mm (2.24in)
Turret top	16mm (.65in)	15mm (.59in)	20mm (.78in)
Turret traverse	Hydraulic/manual	Electric/manual	Hydraulic/manual
Elevation range (degrees)	+20 to -4 degrees	+30 to -3 degrees	+20 to -12.5 degrees
Stabilisation	None	None	None

Sherman Inventory

Type	Total	Began	Ended
M4	6748	July 1942	January 1944
M4A1	6281	February 1942	December 1943
M4A2	8053	April 1942	May 1944
M4A3	1690	June 1942	September 1943
M4A4	7499	July 1942	September 1943
M4A6	75	October 1943	February 1944
M4(105)	1641	February 1944	March 1945
M4A1(76)W	3426	January 1944	July 1945
M4A2(76)W	2915	May 1944	May 1945
M4A3(75)W	3071	February 1944	March 1945
M4A3(76)W	4542	March 1944	April 1945
M4A3(105)	3039	May 1944	June 1945
M4A3E2	254	June 1944	July 1944
All types	49,234	February 1942	July 1945

INDEX